HELPING ADULTS WITH MENTAL RETARDATION GRIEVE A DEATH LOSS

HELPING ADULTS WITH MENTAL RETARDATION GRIEVE A DEATH LOSS*,**

Charlene Luchterhand, MSSW
&
Nancy Murphy, M.Ed.

*The term mental retardation is used throughout this book even though other terminology, such as cognitive disability, is considered more current by some people. The intention is to utilize the term that is most descriptive of the people with whom the authors have worked and the most widely recognized by families and professionals from many disciplines. The term mental retardation is used with the utmost respect for adults with this disability.

**All of the pictures in this book were drawn by adults with mental retardation who have experienced a death loss.

USA	Publishing Office:	ACCELERATED DEVELOPMENT
		A member of the Taylor & Francis Group
		325 Chestnut Street
		Philadelphia, PA 19106
		Tel: (215) 625-8900
		Fax: (215) 625-2940
	Distribution Center:	ACCELERATED DEVELOPMENT
		A member of the Taylor & Francis Group
		1900 Frost Road, Suite 101
		Bristol, PA 19007-1598
		Tel: (215) 785-5800
		Fax: (215) 785-5515
UK		Taylor & Francis Ltd.
		1 Gunpowder Square
		London EC4A 3DE
		Tel: 0171 583 0490
		Fax: 0171 583 0581

HELPING ADULTS WITH MENTAL RETARDATION GRIEVE A DEATH LOSS

1 2 3 4 5 6 7 8 9 0   G H B   9 0 9 8

This book was set in Times Roman. Editing by Cindy Long. Technical development by Thaisa Y. Tiglao. Cover design by Marja Walker.

A CIP catalog record for this book is available from the British Library.
⊗ The paper in this publication meets the requirements of the ANSI Standard Z39.48-1984 (Permanence of Paper)

Library of Congress Cataloging-in-Publication Data available from the publisher.

ISBN 1-56032-768-5 (paper)

Special thanks to my husband, Randy, who shared his technical computer expertise, his time to provide any support activities that were needed, and his continual encouragement.

Charlene

With thanks to my husband, Bob, for his patience, steadfast support, and inspiration.

Nancy

CONTENTS

PREFACE   ix
ACKNOWLEDGMENTS   xi
INTRODUCTION   xv

CHAPTER 1
TYPICAL GRIEVING   1

  Tasks of Mourning   2
  Grief Reactions   6
  Duration of Grieving   13
  Grief Triggers   14

CHAPTER 2
WHAT IS UNIQUE FOR ADULTS
WITH MENTAL RETARDATION?   15

  Common Circumstances of Adults with
    Mental Retardation   15

CHAPTER 3
ESSENTIAL INGREDIENTS IN ASSISTING
ADULTS WITH MENTAL RETARDATION
THROUGH THE GRIEF PROCESS   27

   Actions to Take   28

CHAPTER 4
A MENU OF STRATEGIES TO ASSIST ADULTS
WITH MENTAL RETARDATION ON THEIR
JOURNEY THROUGH GRIEF   37

   How to Use This Chapter   37
   Organization of Menu Ideas   40
   Menu Ideas   43

CHAPTER 5
PROFESSIONAL ASSISTANCE   99

   Warning Signs to Determine When to Seek Help   99
   Indications That Professional Assistance Is Needed 103
   Where to Go for Professional Assistance   103

REFERENCES   109
INDEX   113
ABOUT THE AUTHORS   117

PREFACE

This book has grown out of concern for individuals with mental retardation who have experienced the death of a close family member or friend. The book was written for people who want to take an active role in helping adults with mental retardation grieve a death loss and who are searching for creative ideas to help bereaved individuals. The book is designed to be helpful to families, service providers in the fields of aging or developmental disabilities, hospice staff, and mental health practitioners.

ACKNOWLEDGMENTS

Funding for the content development and writing of this book was provided in part by grant #90DDO287 from the U.S. Department of Health & Human Services, Administration on Developmental Disabilities.

We gratefully acknowledge the assistance of the following people who aided us in one or more of the following ways: by participating in a grief work group, sharing menu ideas, reviewing a draft of the manuscript, or providing professional consultation. The book has benefitted from the contribution that each of them has made:

- Maureen Arcand, Disability Consultant, Madison, Wisconsin.

- Susan Babler, Madison, Wisconsin.

- Rick Brooks, Health Promotion Project, Department of Health & Human Issues, University of Wisconsin-Madison.

- John Burczyk, J.D., Reinhart, Boerner, Van Deuren, Norris, & Rieselbach, Madison, Wisconsin.

- Constituent Advisory Committee, Waisman Center on Mental Retardation and Human Development, University of Wisconsin-

Madison. Committee members include adults with developmental disabilities or family members of these adults who desire to improve the quality of life for all adults with developmental disabilities (Carla Cody, Carl Durocher, Rachel Grant, Mildred Hill, Gwen Jensen, Nancy Livingston, Michael Reece, and Brian Young).

- Charles Degeneffe, MSSW, ACSW, previously with Developmental Disability Counseling, Janesville, Wisconsin.

- Kari Elsner, Madison, Wisconsin.

- Laurie Farnan, M.M.T., R.M.T.-B.C., Central Wisconsin Center for D.D./M.R., Madison, Wisconsin.

- Marian Gender, R.N., RSW, Montcalm Center for Behavioral Health, Stanton, Michigan, sister of an adult with D.D.

- Rachel M. Gordon, MSSW, Madison, Wisconsin.

- Kay Griffith, previously with Jefferson Home Health & Hospice, Madison, Wisconsin.

- Beth Haasl, previously with Unity Hospice, Green Bay, Wisconsin.

- Toni Johnson, CTRS, R.F.D.F., Madison, Wisconsin.

- Chris Jones (C.J.), B.S., Community Support Coordinator, Dungarvin, Madison, Wisconsin.

- Stephen E. Jones, Ph.D., Executive Director, R.F.D.F., Madison, Wisconsin.

- Karen Kiener, B.A., M.Div., Chaplain, Central Wisconsin Center for D.D./M.R., Madison, Wisconsin.

- Maggie Krueger, Executive Director, Cerebral Palsy, Inc., Green Bay, Wisconsin.

- Mariellen Kuehn, Ph.D., UAP Associate Director, Waisman Center on Mental Retardation and Human Development, University of Wisconsin-Madison.

- Kim Leggett-Otto, MSSW, CICSW, HospiceCare, Inc., and Mercy Options Comprehensive Mental Health & Addictions Treatment Services, Janesville, Wisconsin, sister of an adult with D.D.

- Ted Lindquist, Chaplain, St. Mary's Hospital Medical Center, Madison, Wisconsin.

- William B. Love, M.S., previously Associate Research Specialist with Waisman Center on Mental Retardation & Human Development, University of Wisconsin-Madison.

- Cindie Maranger, Madison, Wisconsin.

- David Middleton, M.A., Mental Health Counselor, Northern Pines Community Programs, Cumberland, Wisconsin.

- Vicki L. Neuman, B.S., Asst. Director/Management, Waisman Center on Mental Retardation and Human Development, University of Wisconsin-Madison.

- Vickie Normington, Madison, Wisconsin.

- Shaun O'Keefe, M.A., M.S., previously a Chaplain with HospiceCare Inc., Madison, Wisconsin.

- Allan Saugstad, M.Div., Hospice Chaplain, Franciscan Skemp Health Care, LaCrosse, Wisconsin.

- Jim Sehr, Madison, Wisconsin.

- Gary B. Seltzer, Ph.D., Professor of Social Work, Director of Waisman Center Program on Aging & Developmental Disabilities, University of Wisconsin-Madison.

- Barbara Snyder, previously Bereavement Coordinator at Sacred Heart - St. Mary's Hospital Hospice, Rhinelander, Wisconsin.

- Janet Spearman, Program Director, South Carolina Department of Disabilities & Special Needs, Columbia, South Carolina.

- Harvey L. Sterns, Ph.D., Professor of Psychology, Institute for Life-Span Development & Gerontology, The University of Akron, Akron, Ohio.

- Judy Story, B.A., Coordinator of Special Olympics in Middleton and Cross Plains, Wisconsin, parent of an adult daughter with D.D.

- Evelyn Sutton, M.A., The University of Akron RRTC on Aging with Mental Retardation, Akron, Ohio.

- Molly O Tomony, M.A., A.T.R., previously a Registered Art Therapist with Lifeline Community Hospice, Dodgeville, Wisconsin.

- Ellen Trenn, MSW, Coordinator of Social Services, Family Clinic, Institute on Disability and Human Development, University of Illinois at Chicago.

- Marilyn Viehl, M.H.A., Administrator, Franciscan Skemp Home Health Services, LaCrosse, Wisconsin.

- Betty Zeps, M.A., Field Program Assistant, School of Social Work, University of Wisconsin-Madison.

- All of the adults with mental retardation who shared their experiences with us, and the family members and professionals who participated in our workshops on grief.

INTRODUCTION

A severely handicapped man, who is non-verbal, knelt before the opened casket of his friend. He bowed his head as though in prayer, then reached in the casket to touch the corpse. After rubbing the arm of the deceased, he stood and headed toward the pew. After taking four or five steps, he turned and waved goodby. The staff and I had no idea that this man had an understanding of death. (Marquardt, 1989, p. 347)

Marquardt's anecdote poignantly highlights the importance of addressing the topic of death, grief, and bereavement with adults with mental retardation and including them in traditions and rituals surrounding death. As Howell (1989) wrote

> When we work with a client with mental retardation, we must never assume that he "doesn't know" about the loss and the experience of grieving. . . . We must, in fact, proceed on the assumption that he knows about the loss, that he feels it emotionally, and that it affects his physical body and his spiritual center. (pp. 328-329)

The authors have witnessed situations and learned of others in which adults with mental retardation either have not had a chance to grieve the deaths of loved ones or do not seem to recover from the deaths of people who had been close to them. In some situations, the loss is discussed little if at all and symptoms such as crying are absent, yet there are other signs that the person is not as happy or as functional as before the loss. In other cases, people seem obsessed with thoughts of their deceased loved ones. For some people, the loss seems to be contributing to depression and a diminished quality of life.

The authors have seen other adults with mental retardation who have grieved the deaths of loved ones and have healed from their grief so well that they can be role models for the general population. A music therapist related this story of *receiving* support from a man and a woman with mental retardation who are both in their 40s. The music therapist did not attend practice for the Very Special Arts Choir following the death of her aunt. When the two adults with mental retardation learned from their choir director that the music therapist was sad because her aunt had died, they offered the following:

> Is she eating all right? Is she sleeping? Has she had any nightmares yet? Tell her to talk about it a lot; that's how you get it out. Tell her it's O.K. to cry. Is there any music she likes? I like to listen to "Amazing Grace" when I think of my dad. [The man's father is deceased.] Tell her she's my friend and to call me. Have her call me if she wants to talk.

When the music therapist heard about the conversation, she was struck by the ability of these two people to ask important questions about her welfare and to communicate support. Interestingly, their behavior was in contrast to that of many people in the general population who are afraid to ask questions related to a death loss or communicate support for fear that they will say something "wrong" and upset the person who is grieving!

Another example of *receiving* support from a person with mental retardation was related to the authors by a chaplain. The chaplain had spent a great deal of time in establishing a trusting relationship with a young man and helping him with the losses that he had experienced in his life. The man is nonverbal and has severe disabilities related to a near-drowning accident when he was a child. Tragedy then struck the chaplain's life—her father died unexpectedly. The chaplain arranged for a nurse to explain her absence to the man. On her first day back at work, the chaplain was both surprised and touched as she received support from the man rather than giving it. He seemed to understand that she, like him, had suffered a loss and was very sad. He initiated supportive actions towards her, which he had not done previously. The actions were very similar to the ones the chaplain had used as she had provided comfort for him and taught him about death and loss. He touched his chest above his heart, pulled her toward him, hugged her, and touched her hair in a comforting manner.

If people with mental retardation can be so adept at understanding common grief reactions and coping techniques and are able to *offer* support to someone else who is grieving, should they not also be *receiving* it when there is a crisis in their lives? Of course!

This book has been written in response to questions from family members and staff who are looking for concrete ideas that they can use to support someone who is grieving. It is based upon a literature review and the authors' educational background, continued professional development, clinical experiences, clinical research interviews, and discussions with others. The discussions have occurred individually and in groups with adults with mental retardation, their families, and professionals including art therapists, clergy, music therapists, nurses, social workers, psychologists, hospice professionals, and specialists in developmental disabilities.

The goals of this book are threefold:

- to provide information on typical grieving,
- to outline some features unique to adults with mental retardation who are grieving, and

- to provide some concrete ideas that can be used to assist adults with mental retardation as they move through the grief process.

The material included in this book is to help people who have experienced a recent death loss. If there is concern about someone who experienced a death loss several years ago, it may be prudent to consult with a professional experienced in grief and bereavement issues. Refer to chapter 5 entitled, "Professional Assistance."

As you read this book, do not be surprised to find yourself reminiscing about losses in your own life. This is natural and normal. The time that you spend reflecting on your personal experiences will better prepare you to help someone else. If you are currently grieving a death loss yourself, you may find that you will need to allow more time to read the book, or you may want to postpone your reading to a later date. If you postpone your reading, you might want to encourage a friend, family member, or colleague who is not as involved with the subject matter to read the book now.

The expectation is that this book will be used in a variety of ways. Some people will want to use it immediately for an urgent need. Others may want to read it in preparation for helping someone in the future. Some readers may not have a specific loss in mind but will read it to expand their knowledge and skills in this area. This book can be used to meet all of these varying needs. The recommendation is that you carefully read chapters 1, 2, and 3. Chapter 4 has been designed so that you can scan menu items rapidly to locate ideas that seem most helpful to you. Chapter 5 lists resources if you need or desire additional assistance.

Chapter 1

TYPICAL GRIEVING

Only minimal research has been conducted regarding how adults with mental retardation experience the deaths of people close to them. Based upon the authors' clinical experiences and those of other professionals (Deutsch, 1985; Emerson, 1977; Hedger & Dyer Smith, 1993; Howell, 1989; Kauffman, 1994, Kloeppel & Hollins, 1989; McDaniel, 1989; Pima Council on Developmental Disabilities, 1994; Rothenberg, 1994), and the few studies that have been conducted on this topic (Harper & Wadsworth, 1993), the authors believe that adults with mental retardation are more similar to the general population than different in the feelings and other reactions they experience as they grieve and adapt to losses. This chapter describes grieving that is typical in the United States.

People who are grieving intensely can feel as if they are going crazy. Their behavior also may appear unusual to others who do not know that they are grieving and who are unfamiliar with the usual behavior, thoughts, and feelings of adults who are grieving a death loss. By learning what is typical when someone grieves, a helper will be aware of feelings and reactions that are a normal part of the process, will know what to expect, and will understand how feelings can affect behavior (Weizman & Kamm, 1985). The helper then can provide support, reassure the bereaved person that this is a temporary

1

state, explain this behavior to others, if needed, and determine if professional assistance is warranted.

TASKS OF MOURNING

Worden (1982) identified four tasks that must be accomplished in order for a person to complete the process of mourning successfully:

Task I.   To accept the reality of the loss,
Task II.   To experience the pain of grief,
Task III. To adjust to an environment in which the deceased is missing, and
Task IV.   To withdraw emotional energy and reinvest it.

These tasks are not something about which a grieving person is necessarily conscious or aware. They should not be thought of as a list of "things to do." Rather, they are experiences that have been found to be common among individuals as they move successfully through the grief process. There is no specific order in which people accomplish these tasks, although some order is implied. For example, people first will need to understand that a loss has happened before other tasks become apparent. The following descriptions of the tasks will help clarify their meanings.

Task I. To Accept the Reality of the Loss

Initially, a common response to a death is refusing or having difficulty believing that it actually occurred. As people accomplish this task of mourning, they will come to realize that the death did occur, and that the loved one is gone and will not be coming back.

Task II. To Experience the Pain of Grief

Grief involves emotional pain. People are resistant to feeling pain and do many things to avoid it or escape it. They might deny the pain and state that it does not exist. They might search for a medical answer. They might throw themselves into work or a project or travel in attempts to escape the pain. Ironically, when they do any of these things, they do not escape the pain; instead, they prolong the mourning process. If bereaved individuals do not feel and acknowledge the pain, it is likely to stay "smoldering under the surface." They may carry this pain with them throughout life rather than healing from it, and they are at risk for depression. Feeling the pain and expressing grief are important steps along the pathway to recovering from the loss. As Weizman and Kamm (1985) noted

> Unless you have been allowed and helped to feel all your pain no matter how often it recurs or how long it lasts, and also to express it through tears and words, mourning will not run its natural course. (p. 25)

Frequently bereaved individuals experience physical symptoms— examples include aches in the head, stomach, or neck. Sometimes a description of the physical pain or discomfort is a clue or a metaphor that tells what people are feeling emotionally and how they are experiencing the death (Tatelbaum, 1989; Weizman & Kamm, 1985). A metaphor is a word, phrase, or object that symbolizes something different from its usual meaning. Grief therapists work with metaphors frequently as they assist bereaved individuals. For example, a person might report that his throat feels tight; it feels as if there were a lump in the throat and it seems difficult to swallow. This person might be finding it difficult to accept that the death occurred; he is having trouble "swallowing" the news. The problem with his throat is a metaphor for what he is feeling and experiencing. Another person might report feeling tightness in the chest and pain in the vicinity of the heart. Hearing this symptom, someone might wonder if this person is experiencing a heart attack. Although that is possible, more likely the person is |experiencing emotional anguish or sorrow that we can describe as "heartache" or as being "heartbroken." The physical symptom of tightness in the chest is a metaphor for grief.

In a country as culturally diverse as the U.S., it is helpful to remember that what is considered appropriate expression of emotion will vary considerably among different groups of people. The ethnic background, social class, religious beliefs, geographic location, and whether they live in a rural or urban area all can affect the manner in which adults express emotion (Cook & Dworkin, 1992). Some people may not be comfortable expressing emotional distress but may more readily be able to mention a physical symptom such as a headache. Rosenblatt (1988) reported that WASP Americans (white, Anglo-Saxon, Protestants) are more likely to think and express themselves in psychological terms, while some other ethnic groups are more likely to express their grief through physical symptoms. Behaviors that are considered stereotypic WASP American behaviors, such as "self-control" and "bearing suffering in silence," may be very uncharacteristic for members of other cultures. Japanese mourners tend to smile so that others will not be burdened and "may feel intense guilt and shame if they show strong emotions or feel out of control in public, whereas Hispanic cultures value freedom of emotional expression" (Cook & Dworkin, 1992, p. 153). Gender differences in emotional expression tend to occur as well. Staudacher (1991) reported that the majority of men with whom she has worked react to the death of a loved one by keeping their thoughts and feelings to themselves.

Bereaved individuals will need to feel and express their pain in order to heal; however, it is important not to insist that they face their pain. Instead, they can be supported and gently encouraged to express their feelings as they are able to do so. A caring, supportive, nonjudgmental presence may help them express emotions more easily than any prodding. Helpers will be wise to recognize and understand cultural and ethnic differences in grieving. They then will be less likely to compound people's misery by encouraging them to express grief in ways that are alien to them. As Rosenblatt (1993) said

> It pays to treat everyone as though he or she were from a different culture. The cross-cultural emphasis, in fact, is a kind of metaphor. To help effectively, we must overcome our presuppositions and struggle to understand people on their own terms. (p. 18)

Task III. To Adjust to an Environment
in Which the Deceased Is Missing

This task is unique to each relationship. Different people will need to adjust to differing circumstances. Most people will need to adjust to the loss of companionship and the emotional support they had received from the loved one. Others will need to adjust as well to the loss of activities that the other person performed. This might mean that someone else now has to prepare meals, mow the lawn, provide transportation, and make appointments. There may no longer be anyone who tells them each morning that they are loved or who buys them special gifts. Common for everyone is the need to adapt to change. Some people will learn new skills; others will identify people who can assist them with the various activities that need to be accomplished in life.

Task IV. To Withdraw Emotional Energy
and Then Reinvest It

During the final task of grieving, people will move on with their lives. This can be a very difficult task because bereaved persons initially might feel disloyal to the deceased. The bereaved will need to trust that they will not forget the loved ones who died. The deceased will remain in their hearts and minds forever. Instead of dwelling on the deceased, however, people who are successful with this task will be able to channel their energy into activities and/or other relationships.

Completion of Tasks Is Necessary for Healing

In order to heal from a death loss, each person will accomplish these four tasks in a unique way. Some do so calmly and quietly, saving strong emotion for times when they are alone. Others are more obviously distressed. The manner in which adults grieve can be influenced by such factors as gender, family or cultural traditions, nature of their relationship with the person who died, and previous experiences with death or other crises or stressors in life. There seems to be one commonality—if one or more of the four tasks identified by Worden is not completed, a person is likely to become "stuck" in grief and will not fully heal from the loss. Unresolved grief can resurface later in life and be a significant cause of distress for grieving persons and others around them (Feil, 1993).

Various reasons exist as to why some people do not heal from their losses. Some people do not receive help to heal from their losses. This book was written to prevent this situation from occurring for adults with mental retardation. Others think or act in ways that prevent them from completing the tasks necessary for healing. For example, someone might not accept that the loved one has died; this can occur especially if there has been an accident or violent death in which the body has not been recovered or viewed by the bereaved. Others might feel disloyal to the deceased if they make significant changes in their lives, such as remarrying, moving, or developing new routines. It can be difficult to interact with someone who remains in a chronic state of grief. Yet a helper must accept that not everyone will take the steps necessary to completely work through grief. It is important to respect these individuals and their current coping abilities and circumstances.

GRIEF REACTIONS

Many people have described the major reactions that someone can have when grieving. Psychiatrist Erich Lindemann, M.D., was one of the first to investigate the subject of grieving. His work still is considered to be one of the leading authorities on the subject. J. William Worden and Therese Rando are two other major contributors to the field. The reactions listed below are from the work of these three specialists (Lindemann, 1944; Rando, 1993; Worden, 1982).

Someone might have just one reaction or several in combination. These reactions may appear very strong for awhile and then decrease, or they may appear in moderation but last for a long time. For information on warning signs that show the need for professional help, see chapter 5, "Professional Assistance." You will find a handout listing the reactions and feelings that many adults experience following a death loss in Figure 1.1.

Sadness

Sadness is a typical reaction to a death loss and may or may not include crying. Someone may be very sad and yet be unable or unready to shed tears. It will be helpful to give the person permission to grieve in whatever way is needed.

Anger

In grief, people can experience stronger emotions and may have more difficulty controlling them. Bereaved persons may react quickly and with more intensity than usual. Many individuals experience anger after a death loss, which may result in verbal outbursts, inappropriate behavior, or general irritability. One man with mental retardation who lived in a group home expressed repeatedly how nothing was right after the death of his mother. The food wasn't right; his clothes weren't right, things didn't go well at work. He was sad and angry about his mother's death, and these feelings were conveyed through his complaints about other facets of his life.

Guilt

Guilt may accompany a grief reaction. People can feel guilty that they were not nicer to their loved ones or that their last interactions may not have been pleasant. They may have wished that the loved ones would die or go away and later feel very guilty when the person actually died. Guilt can occur particularly if people believe that they were somehow responsible for the death. If they were in no way responsible for the death, this is called "magical thinking," an erroneous belief that one action can cause an unrelated action. In such situations, it is important to help people understand that they did not cause the deaths to happen.

Because grief can be so painful and sometimes overwhelming, it can cause people to feel frightened and confused, and can result in reactions that can be alarming. Many people worry that they are reacting in the "wrong" way and wonder if there is a "right" way to grieve. There is no "right" way to grieve. Many different expressions of grief are considered normal. If you are concerned or worried about your or another person's reactions to a death loss, you may want to seek counseling or seek out a support group or friend where you can discuss your concerns.

It is helpful to know some of the reactions and feelings that many people have felt after a death loss. They may include the following:

- Body complaints such as sighing, breathing difficulties, heaviness in the chest, tightness in the throat, lack of strength, and exhaustion.

- Changes in sleeping patterns—unable to sleep, sleeping all the time, or going to sleep only to wake early and be unable to return to sleep. Dreams may include the person who has died or events leading up to the death.

- Changes in eating patterns—experiencing a loss of appetite or a desire to eat constantly to help with feelings of emptiness.

- Taking on some of the characteristics of the person who died, such as the way he or she talked or held his or her head, or eating a food he or she enjoyed.

- Feeling separate and cut off from the rest of the world.

- Feeling irritable, restless, and anxious without knowing why.

- Unable to concentrate and/or remember things.

- Unable to stay motivated to do the things that need to be done.

- Fearful of being alone or with people, afraid to leave the house, afraid to stay in the house, or afraid to sleep in the bed.

- Wanting to talk about the person who died over and over again.

- Wanting to spend a lot of time thinking about the person who died, even when it interferes with things that have to be done.

- Feeling angry or guilty at the deceased for leaving.

- Getting angry suddenly and acting in ways not typical.

- Cutting off feelings as a way of coping with something that feels too much to handle right now.

- Getting sick more often than usual due to the stress of experiencing the loss.

- Using alcohol or drugs to help cope with the loss.

- Turning toward God or a spiritual belief for support, or turning away feeling that God or the spiritual support failed.

Figure 1.1.   Reactions to grief and bereavement.

Another type of guilt that people can experience is "survivor guilt" (Simos, 1979). We sometimes read about this type of guilt in the newspapers following a disaster such as an air crash. Survivors might wonder why the victims died and they lived. Sometimes older people experience it when they hear about the deaths of young children. They wonder why they are still living, but a young child has died. A 23-year-old woman with Down syndrome seemed to express similar sentiments when she talked about the death of a neighbor who was a college student. "He was Mr. Perfect. He was smart. He went to college. He had a girlfriend. I do everything wrong; I should have died instead of him."

Prolonged guilt may require professional help.

Somatic Distress

Somatic distress is the physical reaction to emotional stress. It is not unusual for those experiencing a death loss to feel tightness in the throat, dry mouth, heaviness on the chest, persisting weariness in the arms and legs, a sense of emptiness, headaches, stomachaches, over-sensitivity to noise, slight dizziness or faintness, and a pervading sense of exhaustion. They also may sigh frequently. Appetite and sleep disturbances occur frequently. Sometimes a bereaved person may experience somatic distress similar to the physical symptoms that were reported by the deceased before death. This occurs especially if the relationship was a close one and the deceased died after an illness.

Restless Overactivity

Some people react to a death loss with a strong sense of restlessness. They often cope with this feeling by staying very busy. Lots of tasks, walking long distances, and pacing are common.

Feeling Different from Others

It is common to feel quite different and apart from others after a death loss. People's lives may feel so strongly changed, their emotions so raw, and their concentration so poor, that their lives feel very different from those around them.

Appearance of Traits of the Deceased

The person may take on characteristics or habits of the one who has died, such as holding the head in a certain way, using expressions that the deceased had used, or dressing in a similar way. If the grieving person begins to exhibit some of the physical symptoms of the person who died, it may be a good idea to seek some assistance from a professional. See chapter 5, "Professional Assistance."

Regression

There is a tendency for people to regress when a loved one dies. People may feel anxious and helpless about the death and retreat into previous patterns of behavior.

Loss of Daily Routine

It is very common for grieving persons to lose track of their normal routines, particularly in the initial phases of grief. Many normal life activities can be affected, such as daily eating schedules, work assignments, and recreational habits. The more difficult or complex the activity, the more likely it will be for people to have trouble completing it. These tasks or activities can be difficult to remember, or people may lose their concentration or lack energy for them.

Experience with the Image of the Deceased

It is not unusual for some persons to have experiences in which they think that they see or hear the deceased, have a sense of the presence of the deceased, or dream of the person regularly. Although many people experience this, they often do not talk about it until someone else shares a similar experience. Not sharing such experiences and therefore not learning that they are common can contribute to the worry that many bereaved persons have that they are going "crazy."

A South Carolina man in his 30s with mental retardation had such an experience in which he saw and heard his deceased mother. The man was living with his grandmother following the death of his mother. His entire life had become disrupted. He was crying a great deal, was eating little, and his sleep was disturbed. Late one night his grandmother tried to direct him back to bed when she found him wandering around the house. He was insistent that he needed to locate his sunglasses because of a bright light that was hurting his eyes. He later described seeing and hearing his mother. She told him that she was O.K. and that he would be O.K. too. She told him that he needed to continue on with his life and told him to be good. Following this experience, the man started adjusting to his great loss. He returned to work and was able to resume his daily activities.

Some people interpret such reports as evidence that there is life after death. Others believe that the minds of bereaved individuals help them see and hear what they need to help them heal during intense periods of grief. There are probably other explanations as well. Regardless of what one believes, the indisputable fact is that a number of people do have such experiences (Tatelbaum, 1980). The South Carolina man's story is remarkably similar to those reported by a variety of bereaved individuals.

Spiritual Searching/Questioning

Grollman (1996) called attention to another effect of grieving. Spiritual beliefs often are challenged following a death. A grieving person may ask questions similar to the following: Why has God taken this person from me? Who am I apart from this relationship? What meaning does my life have now that this person has died? What do I truly believe happens to a person after death? At this time there is a need for support from others. Rituals, such as visitation, a funeral, and a committal service are frequently helpful.

DURATION OF GRIEVING

There is no definite time line for the length of grieving (Rando, 1993; Worden, 1982); rather, it depends on a wide number of factors that include how the deceased died, the relationship with the person who died, the emotional and social supports of the bereaved, other recent losses, the health and coping methods of the bereaved person, and the meaning or lack of it attached to the death.

In the U.S., the length of time it takes to adjust to a death loss is grossly underestimated and unrecognized. The myth that people can return to work fully functioning after a few days of bereavement leave, or be "back to their old selves" in a few weeks, adds an extra stressor to the bereaved person. Expectations from family members, friends, coworkers, supervisors, and some professionals to be "done" with grieving within a few months does not acknowledge the upheaval of grief and grieving. In the past, traditions such as wearing a black arm band for a year after the death of a loved one meant that the person who died was honored and that others had a visible way to identify the bereaved, who would not "be themselves" for a long while after the death.

Sensitivity to and support for the person who has had a death loss is important for at *least* the first year after the death. A widely accepted myth is that grief and mourning are over in a year. A year usually does mark the end of many "firsts," as in the first holiday season, the first spring, etc.; however, many people find that the second year has its own difficulty as the reality of the death becomes even more final. Deits (1988), a Methodist minister and pastoral counselor, has identified points during the period of mourning that are of special significance for many people: 3 months, 6 to 9 months, 12 months, and 18 months following the loss. At 3 months, the full impact of the loss may be affecting the person. Between 6 and 9 months, the natural immune system may be diminished and the bereaved may be more vulnerable to physical illnesses. The anniversary date at 12 months may be a time for both sadness and hopefulness for the future. At 18 months, some people experience what seems to them to be a relapse of grief. They realize that they are not yet done grieving. Pastor Deits noted that this "bump in the road to recovery" is actually a sign of progress, not regression; it does not last long, and can be handled best by doing the things one would do as if the loss were a recent one. Over time, and with adequate support, the grief reaction usually subsides. Some grief reactions may occur many years after a death (Rando, 1993).

GRIEF TRIGGERS

Grief from a death loss can be triggered, even many years later, by many things, such as special dates (e.g., anniversaries or birthdays), new losses that remind one of the old losses, developmental changes such as moving into an apartment or a first job without mom or dad to witness the event, activities or locations that were enjoyed with the deceased, and seasonal changes, particularly spring and fall. At these times, emotions regarding the death loss resurface and behaviors may change for a while.

Chapter 2

WHAT IS UNIQUE FOR ADULTS WITH MENTAL RETARDATION?

Chapter 1 describes characteristics of grief and bereavement that are common to most individuals in the U.S. Adults with mental retardation also have some characteristics and experiences that are distinct from the general population. These characteristics and experiences can affect how they grieve and how other people perceive or interpret their grief responses. An interesting point to note is that much of what is identified as being unique to adults with mental retardation actually relates more to the actions of others than to characteristics or actions of the adults with mental retardation themselves. For example, others may treat adults with mental retardation differently because of their diagnosis of mental retardation.

COMMON CIRCUMSTANCES OF ADULTS WITH MENTAL RETARDATION

This chapter describes some common themes that are seen in adults with mental retardation. Again, people are individually different; that is, not all adults with mental retardation will exhibit all of these characteristics nor have all of these experiences. Some ways in which adults with mental retardation may differ from their peers in the general population include the following:

1. difficulties in learning or understanding (cognitive difficulties);
2. decreased or altered expression of emotion;
3. tendency to respond in a positive manner;
4. behavior (rather than words) is indicative of true feelings;
5. often family members or professionals treat them differently from others;
6. family members or professionals often act as reporters or interpreters;
7. lack of social support;
8. sense of connection to others that is not obvious;
9. history of multiple losses;
10. lack of resources; and/or
11. uncertain future.

Difficulties in Learning or Understanding (Cognitive Difficulties)

Difficulty in learning or understanding is one of the major reasons why some family members and professionals do not talk about death with adults who have mental retardation. Others assume that adults with mental retardation will not understand what has happened. In the past, many people believed that children could not understand the concept of death either, yet now there are a variety of books designed to teach children about death. Bowlby (1980) reported on the work of Robert and Erna Furman. They found that even a child no older than two can understand that death is irreversible and can occur because of natural causes. The key to the child's understanding is what he or she is told and whether or not this information is consistent with his or her experiences. For example, if a child is told that it is natural to feel sad and to wish we could bring the person back again, he or she will feel understood because this is likely to be how the child is feeling.

The cognitive abilities of adults with mental retardation vary greatly from person to person. It may be quite difficult to know for certain how someone who has severe or profound mental retardation is experiencing loss. However, most adults with mental retardation have mild or moderate cognitive disabilities. They will have emotions about a death and will have the ability to understand and talk about this issue (to the extent that any of us understands and accepts the concept). They will benefit from assistance in learning about death, loss, and possible reactions to expect during grief. As Tatelbaum (1980) noted when speaking about human beings in general, "it is our lack of knowledge about grief that increases our fear, despair, hopelessness, and helplessness when we face a major loss in our lives" (p. 11).

It is critical for helpers to realize also that adults with mental retardation do not have to understand the concept of death to feel loss. They are likely to experience loss and grief if people previously close are no longer in their lives. This will happen regardless of their understanding of death. It is the *experience of loss* and subsequent grief about that loss, not whether or not the adults with mental retardation are likely to understand the concept of death, that should motivate others to provide assistance. Over time these adults may come closer to an understanding of death. For example, as time goes on and the loved ones do not return, adults with mental retardation may come closer to understanding that death is forever—a concept that they might not have understood when the deaths first occurred.

To summarize this section, the greatest dilemma is not that some adults have cognitive difficulties because of mental retardation. Rather, the real problem occurs when helpers immediately assume that adults with mental retardation will not feel the loss, that they need to be protected from the truth, or that by not talking about the issue, the loss will be less poignant for them. Then the source of obtaining the very help they need is cut off before the helping process can begin.

Decreased or Altered Expression of Emotion

Many adults with mental retardation do not express their emotions in the manner typical of adults, particularly when the emotions they have are not positive. Their faces and words may not express their true feelings. For example, they may show a pleasant or neutral face to the outside world when inside they are hurting. This may be particularly true of older adults with mental retardation who may not have received training about emotions or who may have experienced unpleasant consequences when they did share all of their emotions. In working with individuals with mental retardation, it may be important to look for other indicators of their true emotions, such as their behavior, and to use nonverbal means of helping them express their emotions. (See chapter 4 for ideas.)

Tendency to Respond in a Positive Manner

Some persons with mental retardation have a tendency to respond affirmatively to whatever question is asked (Sigelman, Budd, Winder, Schoenrock, & Martin, 1982). For example, they may be sad or angry, but they will report that they are happy. (See Figures 2.1 and 2.2.) They may do this because they have developed over the years a desire to please the person with whom they are interacting and respond in a socially desirable way, or they may feel uncertain about the consequences of giving a response that appears to be negative. For example, if they say that they are angry, what will happen? Will someone, in turn, be angry with them? Will they have to see a psychiatrist? Will they have to move?

Behavior (Rather Than Words) Is Indicative of True Feelings

For some adults with mental retardation, a change in behavior may be a better indicator that they are upset than their affect and words. Emerson, a consultant in the field of developmental disabilities, often worked with families or residential agencies when someone with mental retardation developed uncharacteristic behaviors such

Figure 2.1. Some adults with mental retardation tend to respond in a positive manner even when sad. The artist drew her family members following a death. Note the smiles on their faces.

Figure 2.2. The artist's response to the question, "How do the people feel inside?"

as verbal or physical aggression or extreme withdrawal. She reported that 50% of these clients had experienced either the death or the loss of someone close preceding the onset of symptoms (Emerson, 1977).

Behavior to observe includes the following:

- Have sleeping patterns changed?
- Is the bereaved person sleeping more or less than usual?
- Is sleep disturbed?
- Have eating habits changed?
- Has work productivity changed?
- Is the person withdrawing from social activities?
- Has there been an increase in the number or severity of physical symptoms exhibited?
- Have any personality characteristics changed? For example, has a usually mild-mannered individual had some verbal outbursts?

One man who lived in a group home in a rural community changed inexplicably from being a quiet, gentle person to having episodes in which he was loud, impatient, and demanding. Staff who worked with him were very puzzled about this change. After repeated efforts to determine the cause of the change, the man revealed to one staff member than he was very angry that his mother had died eight months earlier. Because he never spoke about her, cried, or gave other indications that he was upset, staff had assumed that he already had coped with her death and had recovered from this loss.

Many behaviors that are normal for someone who is grieving are similar to symptoms of someone who is depressed. If the person continues over time to experience changes in sleeping or eating patterns and withdrawal from activities that previously were enjoyable, professional assistance should be sought to determine if the person is clinically depressed.

Often Family Members or Professionals
Treat Them Differently from Others

Many times adults with mental retardation are treated as if they were children. People often try to shield them from the harsh realities of life and death. One adult family home provider reported that he was not planning to tell the woman who lived with him that her mother was dying. Furthermore, he had no intention of informing her about the death when it occurred. "Parts of her life have been very difficult," he said. "I want her to have only happy days." He meant well; however, people with mental retardation do not live in a vacuum. Their lives will be affected by the death of someone close to them. When they are treated differently because they have mental retardation, they may have additional burdens with which they must cope. Some individuals have found out about the deaths of family members by reading the obituary column in the newspaper or by overhearing someone talking about it in the community. They may have been left out of family gatherings or rituals surrounding the death, such as funerals. They then may need assistance to cope with their feelings of isolation or anger at being left out, as well as their grief. They may feel that death is a taboo subject or that they have to protect the feelings of other family members by not talking about it. A man in his 30s expressed great emotion about the death of his aunt, as he spoke with one of the authors. His aunt clearly had been an important person in his life. He found out about her death by reading the paper; there was no mention of it in his home. During the conversation, he initially begged the author not to tell his mother. No one at his home apparently knew the extent to which he was grieving and doing so alone, and he did not want to upset them by bringing up the subject.

Family Members or Professionals Often
Act as Reporters or Interpreters

Some adults with mental retardation are not reliable reporters; that is, they have difficulty remembering or reporting details accurately.

Others do not have verbal skills necessary for someone who does not know them well to understand their conversation. Family members or other caregivers can provide a valuable service by acting as a reporter to share important facts about the person's past history or as an interpreter to help others know what the adult with mental retardation is trying to communicate. However, there is a danger with this situation as well. The helper may misinterpret the person's feelings and experiences. This may be especially true regarding issues of grief and bereavement, since many helpers will be unfamiliar with characteristics of typical grieving and uncomfortable with the subject (Kloeppel & Hollins, 1989).

It is important whenever an interpreter or reporter is used to ask detailed questions rather than just obtaining the helper's beliefs. For example, if you are a parent who is concerned about how your son who lives in a group home is coping with a death, do not ask staff *if* your son is coping with the death; instead ask for details. Questions to ask might include the following:

- *How* has he responded when staff have talked to him about the person who died?
- *What* has he done or said that makes staff think he is coping well or not coping well?
- Has he acted in ways that are unusual for him?

Lack of Social Support

Many people who have worked with adults with mental retardation have been surprised by the intensity of emotion expressed many years after a death. Some individuals talk about a death that occurred as long as 10 years ago as if it were a recent event. This has been a perplexing phenomenon. The authors' perspective is that some people have not worked through the grief process thoroughly and have become "stuck" in their grief. Among people with whom the authors have worked, it appears that the death of a parent, in particular, is related to this phenomenon. In some ways this should not be surprising. In general, adults with mental retardation have smaller social support systems than their peers who do not have mental retardation. Most do not marry or have children or grandchildren; some have limited opportunities to develop friendships. Staff turnover in agencies that provide residential support is frequently high. The relationships that are the closest in their entire lives may be their relationships to their parents. Thus, grieving the death of a parent for them may require much more time, effort, and support than for bereaved individuals in the general population.

Sense of Connection to Others That Is Not Obvious

Some family members or professionals are surprised at the intensity of the grief expressed by someone with mental retardation, because they did not feel that the relationship had been a close one. For example, perhaps a woman reacted strongly to the death of an aunt who had never appeared close to her. Again, remember the relatively small social circle of adults with mental retardation. These adults may fear being left alone in the world without relatives. As a woman with Down syndrome in her 30s reported as she worried about conflict among extended family members, "I have people dying left and right in my family; I have to keep the rest of them together." Also, relationships with adults with mental retardation may not involve the same give-and-take when compared to other relationships, yet to the adult with mental retardation the relationship is an important one. The brother of a woman with mental retardation who participated in a sibling focus group reported feeling astounded when he realized how close his sister felt to him. He did not have the same type of relationship with her as with other important people in his life. Her feelings of connection to him had not been readily apparent.

History of Multiple Losses

Be aware that many older adults with mental retardation have experienced multiple losses over the years. They may have had numerous residential transitions, losses of friends with whom they had lived, staff turnover, and changes in jobs and vocational settings. If the person who died was the primary caregiver of the adult with mental retardation, multiple losses (such as living arrangements, daily routines, availability of support and attention, and financial circumstances) may occur all at once (Kloeppel & Hollins, 1989). Another situation resulting in multiple losses occurs when a recent loss re-awakens feelings related to a loss that someone experienced earlier in life. Grief can become more complicated when someone experiences such multiple losses. The bereaved individual may be overwhelmed and not able to complete the "grief work" necessary to heal without assistance.

Lack of Resources

Adults with mental retardation may lack knowledge or skills that would enable them to cope better with their losses. They may not have been exposed to death before or had training that would enable them to understand better what occurs. Frequently they lack the resources or abilities to carry out actions that they feel would be helpful. For example, most do not have driver's licenses or their own cars. If they want to visit a cemetery, they may need to rely on public transportation or the understanding and goodwill of family members or staff. They may not have money to take a vacation or the ability to arrange a trip so that they could "get away from it all" for a brief time, as many people in the general population do when they feel stressed.

Uncertain Future

Most adults with mental retardation need some form of lifelong support. If that support had been supplied previously by the person who died, the future may appear to them to be like a big, black hole, and very frightening. Whether the relationship between the adult with mental retardation and the deceased was an obviously close one or a "hidden connection," the death can increase fear that others in the bereaved person's life will die soon. This can help cause the person to feel that the world is unpredictable, out of control, and unsafe.

It will be helpful to keep these characteristics and experiences in mind as you work with an adult with mental retardation. They may provide clues regarding why someone is behaving in a certain way, what emotions are being felt, and how you might assist.

Chapter 3

ESSENTIAL INGREDIENTS IN ASSISTING ADULTS WITH MENTAL RETARDATION THROUGH THE GRIEF PROCESS

Two very important procedures are to tell persons with mental retardation about the deaths of people close to them and allow them time to grieve. All too often, adults with mental retardation are not told about the deaths of people close to them. When they are told, families and professionals feel uncertain about how to help them with their grief. Sometimes, caregivers try to distract them so that they will not cry or show other strong emotion, erroneously assuming that if they do not cry, then they are not upset about the death. Yet, as you learned in chapter 1, certain tasks of mourning must be completed if people are to successfully grieve the deaths of people close to them. As stated previously, the authors believe that adults with mental retardation will need to accomplish the same tasks of mourning as does the general population.

ACTIONS TO TAKE

Much of the support given to someone who is grieving is unique to that person and the particular situation. Yet some actions will be helpful to most adults with mental retardation whom you are supporting through the grief process. Helpers may want to consider the following guidelines:

- tell the person that the death has occurred,
- allow and encourage the person to share his or her feelings,
- provide reassurance that he or she is not alone and that others are there to help,
- remember that the grief process takes time,
- be patient with the grieving person, and
- learn from the person who is grieving.

Tell the Person That the Death Has Occurred

Some people debate whether or not an adult with mental retardation should be told about the illness and death of someone close to them. In contrast, the authors believe that adults with mental retardation should participate as full citizens in the community. They then cannot be denied the opportunities to learn about life and death events that affect them intimately. To do so would be to not allow them the full range of human experiences. Lotte Moise (1978), the mother of a daughter with mental retardation, described it well:

> How fully do we let our children experience this full range of emotions? And how can we honestly interpret their total humanness to others, if we, their parents, are less than honest with them? And honesty includes our preparing them for sickness and dying. They deserve no less than this. (p. 398)

Two other major reasons exist for openness regarding death. First, adults with mental retardation will know that something is wrong; something will be different in their lives. No one provides transportation to visit mom in the nursing home. A new staff person arrives unexpectedly, and no one talks about the previous staff member who seemed to vanish. Grandma no longer sends gifts or comes to visit. When changes such as these happen without explanation, people are likely to use their imagination to fill in the missing information. Their imagination might provide worse explanations than reality. "Mom doesn't love me anymore." "I did something wrong, so my favorite staff person is mad at me and won't spend time with me anymore." "Grandma was sick when I saw her. She died and I'm going to die too because I will catch what she had."

The other reason for being open with adults with mental retardation is that they will be better prepared to cope with the death if they learn about it in a direct way. Bowlby (1980) stated, "There seems little doubt that the more direct the knowledge the less tendency is there for disbelief that death has occurred to persist" (p. 182).

If news of a death has been kept secret, it is natural that the bereaved person will believe that the loved one will return some day. Bowlby reported that faulty or false information at the time of death frequently will mean that people are not able to grieve consciously. They then will be at risk for more complicated grief reactions.

The following are suggestions for telling an adult with mental retardation about the death of someone close.

Identify Another Person Who Is Close Or One Who At Least Knows and Is Familiar with the Adult with Mental Retardation to Break the News about the Death. If such a person is readily available, it can help in easing the pain and shock of receiving the distressing news.

Carefully Choose the Initial Statement and the Setting Where the Person Is Told about the Death. Following are some suggestions:

- Use a cushioning statement. For example, "I have some sad news to tell you," or "I have some news that's hard for me to tell you."
- Suggest going to a quiet place to talk.
- Ask the person if there is someone whom he or she would like to have present.
- Allow the person to flee the room if he or she needs to do so. Some people feel a need to get away from the place where they heard bad news and from the person who has given them this news. This person may want to be with someone after he or she has had a chance to absorb the news.

Explain the Death in a Way That Maximizes the Person's Ability to Understand. There is no "right way" to tell a person about the death of someone close. Each situation is unique, and each interaction will be unique. There is a wide range of knowledge and experiences related to death and loss among adults with mental retardation. Some adults have experienced previous death losses; others might have been sheltered from the concept. Use your knowledge of a person and your relationship with that person to help you tell him or her what happened. The following suggestions highlight some issues to keep in mind.

- Explain the death using words that you think he or she will understand.
- Use concrete images rather than abstract concepts. For example, say, "Do you remember how sick Grandma looked when we saw her last week? The doctors were not able to help her get better and she died," rather than "Grandma passed away."
- Be open, direct, and honest.
- Try to avoid phrases that can have multiple meanings. Say, "She died," rather than, "She went to 'sleep,'" or "She 'flew up' to heaven." If words with more common meanings are used, someone might later show a fear of that activity. For example, the person may be afraid to fall asleep or fly in an airplane.

- Invite questions and answer them honestly.
- Use examples that the person already may have encountered: a pet dying, a wild animal or bird dying, a plant dying. (See Figure 3.1.)

Do Not Fret If You Happen to Say Something in a Manner That Was Not Ideal. The person's ability to recover from the loss is not dependent on your doing and saying everything in a perfect manner at one specific point in time. Grieving is a process. The person will be helped over time and probably by several people. If an adult with mental retardation has a misperception about the death, he or she can be helped over time to understand more fully what has occurred.

Allow and Encourage the Person to Share His or Her Feelings

Family members and other care providers sometimes become upset by the amount and the intensity of the emotion that is initially expressed by an adult with mental retardation. They may try to prevent a strong show of emotion such as crying or angry outbursts. This is understandable; it is very difficult to watch someone else grieve, particularly if the person has been sheltered from adult problems. Yet openly expressing the pain will help the person recover. Generally, the strong emotional response will subside over time. If the grief response is overwhelming to you, professional assistance or consultation is available.

Some individuals who have experienced the death of someone close to them have the opposite response. They do not appear upset and seem quite calm; they do not talk about the death. They may be coping in their own ways. However, be aware that the adult with mental retardation may not yet fully realize the impact of the death— that the loved one will *never* return. It may take several months to feel the loss. Sometimes adults with mental retardation can have an uncharacteristic behavior change many months after the death. The

Figure 3.1.   When asked to draw a picture of someone close who died, the artist drew her dog.

authors suggest that most adults with mental retardation would benefit from having someone who will initiate conversation about the death. It is not a good idea, though, to force the person to interact with you about the subject. Instead, offer the *opportunity* to talk with you about it on several occasions over a period of time, at least several months.

Provide Reassurance That He or She Is Not Alone and That Others Are There to Help

Evidence is available to suggest that whether bereaved individuals feel that others are helpful or not helpful during the grief period can influence how successfully they recover from the death (Bowlby, 1980).

One reason why people avoid talking about a death is that they do not know what to say or what to do. They feel helpless. They know that they cannot solve the problem, because the problem is death and death is irreversible. People who are grieving also may ask questions that are difficult to answer or which have no answers. For example, *why* did my loved one die? Why did this happen *now*? What will happen to me?

As a helper, you need to realize that you are not expected to solve the problem. You cannot change history; you cannot reverse the fatal car crash or cure the cancer that killed a loved one. You also cannot take the pain away from the person who is grieving.

You *can* learn how to comfort someone who is experiencing emotional pain. You can be there so that the adult with mental retardation is not alone. You can listen. You can give a hug. You can hold a hand. You can do an activity or arrange for someone else to do an activity that was done previously by the deceased with the person. You can reassure him or her that someone will be there in the future. It may help to spend some time helping the bereaved person identify people to whom he or she might turn for help of various kinds. For example, who could give the person with mental retardation a ride to church? Who would go out to dinner with him or her? To whom could he or she talk when feeling sad or lonely? Weizman and Kamm (1985) noted that a grieving person needs help and support for a longer time than the usual social and religious practices related to death in our culture would indicate.

Remember That the Grief Process Takes Time

As you learned in chapter 1, people differ in the length of time during which they feel grief acutely. It is worth repeating: grief usually lasts longer than many people expect. The authors have heard caregivers remark now that the funeral was over, people could "put the death behind them and life could get back to normal." In reality, what had been normal is now gone. The bereaved person needs to learn how to live without the loved one. In fact, the adjustment period that we call "grief work" is just beginning.

Be Patient with the Grieving Person

Grieving persons often feel the need to tell and retell anecdotes about their relationship with the person who died and details of the illness and death. This helps them "hear" or come to terms with the reality of what has happened and to adjust to this new reality (Cook & Dworkin, 1992; Weizman & Kamm, 1985). In general, adults with mental retardation have smaller social circles; therefore, the same people are likely to hear the person's story numerous times. Unfortunately, a compassionate listener hearing these stories many times may burn out and eventually shy away from the bereaved person.

Helping professionals may mistake this phenomenon for perseveration in adults with mental retardation. Perseveration is a disturbance in thinking frequently characterized by repeating the same words over and over again. The danger in mistaking the grief symptom of retelling for perseveration is that adults with mental retardation then may receive medication or behavioral intervention inappropriately.

Understanding that "retelling" is a normal part of grieving, and being willing to listen nonjudgmentally to multiple retellings can help the bereaved greatly at a time when their usual support may be getting weary or drifting away.

Learn from the Person Who Is Grieving

Hospice staff and others who work in the field of grief know that one of the most important guidelines to remember in assisting someone who is grieving is to learn from that person. They quickly learn to "walk beside" the grieving person, rather than assuming that they know what the person is feeling and experiencing at any given time or trying to "lead" him or her to a different state of mind. Each person's experience is unique.

You can learn how to help a particular person by watching and listening to the person closely. If you do not do this, it is easy to make erroneous assumptions. A 46-year-old woman with mental retardation showed strong grief reactions whenever staff attempted to talk with her about her mother who had died six months previously. She would become loud, avoid the subject, look for her belongings, and try to leave the room. She also refused to visit the family home where her mother had lived. Yet the staff had been told earlier by one of her sisters that she had not been close to her mother and therefore was not upset about her mother's death. The sister had assumed the woman would have feelings similar to her own and did not recognize the grief symptoms.

The authors have been struck by anecdotes indicating that some adults with mental retardation have known what they need to cope and have tried to enlist the help of others. The authors have heard people with mental retardation ask for rides to cemeteries; have heard people ask for items that previously belonged to deceased loved ones as a way to remember them; have heard a story about one man who, at least 10 years after his mother's death, wanted "to buy her a rose." The staff person whom he asked for help was concerned about this seemingly bizarre behavior and wondered whether she should help him with this request. As she talked with him further, she learned that the behavior was not strange at all. Roses had been his mother's favorite flowers; he wanted to put a rose on her grave for Mother's Day. How sad that he waited over 10 years for a staff person who was able to understand and help him. What a tribute to the human spirit that he persisted and eventually obtained the help he needed!

Chapter 4

A MENU OF STRATEGIES TO ASSIST ADULTS WITH MENTAL RETARDATION ON THEIR JOURNEY THROUGH GRIEF

This section will focus on some specific ideas that families or professionals can utilize as they assist an adult with mental retardation through the grief process.

These ideas have been gleaned from a multitude of sources: surveys of hospice agencies, conversations with families and professionals, literature searches, grief work group meetings, and interviews with adults with mental retardation. Acknowledgment has been given to the original source of these ideas to the extent possible; however, sometimes the idea has been learned secondhand. The authors sincerely apologize if the original source is not adequately acknowledged.

HOW TO USE THIS CHAPTER

This chapter is *not* a grief therapy manual nor a recipe for how to help someone through grief. Rather, this chapter should be thought of as a *menu* of items from which appropriate selections can be chosen, similar to a menu at a restaurant. As you interact with a bereaved person with mental retardation, you undoubtedly will be trying to determine how the person is coping with the death. If the person needs assistance (or if you are unsure that he or she needs assistance) you may want to incorporate some of these ideas into your interactions. The authors believe that most, if not all, adults with mental retardation will benefit from the assistance of someone who will talk openly about the death and the impact of this loss. Some individuals also may need assistance from someone who specializes in grief issues.

Use Helping Techniques Specific to Each Person

If you decide to use some of these ideas, an important step is to pick and choose ideas that seem particularly relevant to the specific person with whom you are interacting. The following two examples will help demonstrate this point.

Example 1. Some adults with mental retardation do not express their true feelings; instead their usual response is "I'm happy" or "I'm fine" even when they are sad, angry, or upset. If you know this is characteristic of the individual, you may want to try some ideas to help the person acknowledge his or her feelings regarding the death (e.g., menu ideas 22, 23, and 26). Also, you may want to try some of these ideas if you do not know the individual well or if there is some indication as you observe the person's behavior that he or she is not expressing true feelings. For instance, perhaps he or she is acting in unusual or inappropriate ways and the onset of the behavior seems to coincide with the death.

Example 2. Several people with mental retardation have reported that they became quite upset at some point after the death because family or staff quit talking about the deceased person. People who are feeling this way might benefit from some of the techniques in this section that are geared toward helping bereaved individuals remember the deceased (e.g., menu ideas 61, 62, and 83).

Use Your Knowledge of the Person to Help You Identify Strategies That Might Be Helpful, but Also Experiment with New Approaches

If someone enjoys arts and crafts, try some techniques that utilize this type of approach. If someone enjoys music, try musical ideas. If religion is important to someone, use some of the religious ideas. However, do not feel that you must restrict yourself to these specific approaches. Perhaps a person who does not usually do artwork will respond very well to an art project. Maybe someone who does not attend church will find comfort in a particular hymn. You should feel free to try a variety of techniques.

Use Your Creativity

These techniques listed are ideas that people have shared that they or others have found helpful. You can use them as a starting point. Feel free to use some of them, not use some, modify others, and create entirely new ideas.

Know Your Own Grief Triggers

As you provide caring support to an adult with mental retardation who is grieving a death loss, you may encounter memories of losses in your own life. Who or what have you lost? How have you mourned? Is there something that seems to trigger grief for you as you attempt to support someone else? If you find that your emotions are stronger than you expected, take time out to examine your own loss history. Try to identify what might be stimulating memories or emotions for you. Perhaps you can use some of the information in this booklet to help yourself heal.

One Last Reminder before You Begin

Please remember that one of the "tasks of mourning" is *to experience the pain of grief.* As you talk about the death and perhaps work on some activities, it is not unusual for the bereaved person initially to look or act more upset than previously. *This may be a good sign—that he or she is feeling comfortable enough to express his or her true emotions and is doing some of the "grief work" necessary for future healing.* If you become very uncomfortable, consult a grief specialist. (Refer to chapter 5.) Specialists should feel free to confer with other specialists.

ORGANIZATION OF MENU IDEAS

The menu ideas have been organized under headings that correspond with Worden's four tasks of grieving, which were described in chapter 1.

Task I.   To accept the reality of the loss.
Task II.   To experience the pain of grief.
Task III. To adjust to an environment in which the deceased is
           missing.
Task IV.   To withdraw emotional energy and reinvest it.

The menu items are placed in this order to help you locate those items that are appropriate for the person at a given time. For example, when a death occurs, the first task is to accept the reality of the loss. Menu items related to the funeral or memorial service will be very appropriate. Introducing the bereaved person to a new hobby would be more appropriate at a later time.

The items are placed roughly in the order that you might use them. Many items can be used as someone is coping with more than one of Worden's tasks. The order should be considered as a guideline, not a rule, since there is a great deal of variation among different people.

Menu items have been identified according to the type of activity involved. This will help you if you are searching for a particular type of idea (e.g., an activity using music). Categories are listed with each menu item. Also an index of menu items by category can be found in Figure 4.1. Some menu items will fall under more than one classification. Categories include the following:

Creative Arts
    8, 26, 30, 32, 35, 44, 53, 57, 63, 64, 66, 67, 69, 71, 79, 87,
    101, 106

Instruct/Teach/Model
    6, 17, 19, 20, 21, 22, 25, 27, 28, 41, 43, 58, 64, 81, 82, 88,
    92, 99, 102, 103

Music
    6, 28, 29, 34, 45, 46, 47, 48, 51, 52, 65, 73, 74, 75, 76, 78,
    104

Nature/Outdoors
    36, 37, 38, 39, 42, 90, 97, 98, 100, 105

Physical
    39, 42, 52, 94, 95, 97, 98, 99, 100

Religious/Spiritual
    4, 5, 6, 7, 9, 10, 11, 12, 16, 31, 33, 34, 80, 85

Ritual/Tradition
    4, 6, 7, 8, 9, 10, 11, 12, 13, 14, 38, 39, 40, 41, 56, 61, 62,
    68, 70, 77, 79, 80, 86, 90, 99, 100, 101, 105, 107

Support from Others
    1, 2, 3, 5, 10, 12, 14, 15, 18, 19, 20, 22, 23, 24, 25, 26, 27,
    28, 31, 32, 33, 42, 43, 48, 49, 50, 51, 54, 55, 58, 59, 60,
    61, 69, 72, 78, 81, 82, 83, 84, 87, 88, 89, 91, 92, 93, 96,
    102

Verbal
    2, 20, 24, 25, 26, 42, 49, 50, 68, 70, 72, 83, 84, 87, 91

Figure 4.1.   Index of menu items by category.

Figure 4.2. A drawing of the artist's father following a fatal heart attack. Note frown and prone position.

Creative Arts—making something with the hands;

Instruct/Teach/Model—learning from someone who will teach, provide instruction, or model a behavior;

Music—listening or performing music;

Nature/Outdoors—engaging in an activity outdoors or one related to nature;

Physical—engaging the body in a physical activity;

Religious/Spiritual—participating in a religious activity or one that is seen as spiritual;

Ritual/Tradition—participating in an activity that is symbolic of feelings and thoughts related to the death or that is customary in one's culture following a death;

Support from Others—receiving words of comfort or other types of assistance from others; and

Verbal—speaking with others about the person who died, the death, and related events.

MENU IDEAS

Task I. To Accept the Reality of the Loss (See Figure 4.2.)

1. *Help the bereaved individual identify and stay overnight in a location that provides the most comfort during the days surrounding the death* (**Support from Others**). If possible, allow the person with mental retardation to choose where to stay. If someone chooses to stay in his or her own apartment, the individual may benefit from others providing more support than usual. Several adults with mental retardation have reported that they needed to be with other family members and wanted to stay at the homes of their parents or siblings for several days. In some cases, these families may be hesitant to offer this arrangement, feeling that being in a grieving household might upset the person with mental retardation. Yet adults with mental retardation might cope better if they are not excluded from the family's interactions at this time.

2. *Identify family members or staff who can speak to the bereaved person about the death openly and honestly* (**Support from Others; Verbal**). This is especially important if there is someone to whom the bereaved person is likely to turn for help but who is unable to speak with the bereaved person openly and honestly about the subject. The mother of a daughter with mental retardation reported that she was very open in talking to her daughter about the subject but knew that the subject of death was very difficult for her daughter's grandparents and that they would not be able to answer her questions in a beneficial way. The daughter was encouraged to talk to the mother when a death occurred in the family. Ideally, more than one person should be identified who can deal with this subject.

3. *Utilize appropriate physical contact* (**Support from Others**). A hand on someone's arm, a pat on the back, holding someone's hand, and a hug can go a long way in conveying support and caring. Be sensitive to the fact that some people have personal boundaries that would make physical contact objectionable for them.

4. *Involve the person in making funeral arrangements* (**Religious/Spiritual; Ritual/Tradition**). The person with mental retardation might help select the clothing the deceased will wear or help choose flowers or music to be played during the funeral or memorial service. Along with other family members, he or she could talk to the clergy who will be officiating at the service to provide anecdotes about the deceased that could be shared during the service.

5. *Provide suggestions for the clergy member who is officiating at a funeral or memorial service regarding how the service might be made more meaningful for the person with mental retardation* (**Spiritual/Religious; Support from Others**). This is particularly important if the person who died was someone very close to the person with mental retardation, such as a parent or a sibling, and if the bereaved person has cognitive disabilities in the severe or profound range.

Some suggestions for enhancing a service for an adult with mental retardation include the following: Allow and encourage the person with mental retardation to respond at the appropriate times with sound in his or her own way. If the individual is nonverbal, the sound may be a tone, noise, or unintelligible singing rather than understandable words. If communion is part of the service and the person is not able to participate in the traditional way, he or she might be allowed to taste or smell the elements rather than eat and drink them. If this is not possible, the clergy might touch his or her head and give a blessing. If members of the family are named during the service, the clergy should take care to name the person with mental retardation along with the other family members.

Utilizing tangible objects and the sense of touch can be very important for the person with severe disabilities. A chaplain who has conducted many services attended by adults with disabilities suggests that a portion of the service be planned around something that can be felt, held, smelled, or even eaten. For example, the chaplain has read the book *The Fall of Freddie the Leaf* (Buscaglia, 1982) and has brought leaves to the service for people to hold. The chaplain brought candles and balloons to a service for a person who was buried on her 21st birthday. People who attended were encouraged to take a candle and balloon home and celebrate the person's life in addition to grieving her death. At a service for a person who was Native American, the chaplain passed around a dish of strawberries and burned sweet grass, which corresponded with the spiritual reading and the deceased's cultural tradition.

6. *Investigate possibilities of allowing the person to participate in the funeral or memorial service* (**Music; Religious/Spiritual; Ritual/Tradition**). In some religious or cultural traditions, family members and friends take part in the service. They may be pallbearers or they may speak at the service, sharing their memories of the person. Someone might hand out song sheets, sing, or play a musical instrument.

Investigate if such possibilities exist, and ask the person with mental retardation if he or she would like to take part. If the person would like to participate but is unable to do so for any reason, you may be able to modify the activity. For example, if someone would like to share his or her memories about a family member but feels too nervous or upset to speak at the service, perhaps you could help him or her write some thoughts down on paper, and the clergy, a family member, or a friend could read the memories out loud at the service.

Several men with Down syndrome have been pallbearers for their grandparents. As one man said, "I was scared and shaking, but I just took a big breath and I did it." He seemed honored that he had been selected as a pallbearer and proud that he was able to do it.

It will be important to explain to the person with mental retardation what will take place during the service and what exactly he or she will be asked to do. Also, when will he or she do the activity, and who can help if a problem should occur?

7. *Offer the opportunity to add something personally meaningful to the funeral or memorial service to honor or remember the person who died* (**Religious/Spiritual; Ritual/Tradition**). Clients of a sheltered workshop in central Wisconsin experienced the unexpected death of one of their members, a young man who appeared in good health but died suddenly one weekend. The case manager was able to get everyone together on Monday, inform them about the death, and ask how they wished to remember this man. The group decided that they wanted to make a banner. They decorated the banner with pictures and words—things the man liked and some of his favorite sayings. They requested and received permission from the family to display the banner at the memorial service.

8. *Help the person create and display a collage of photographs at the visitation, funeral, or memorial service* (**Creative Arts; Ritual/Tradition**). Gather photographs depicting the deceased at different stages in life. Help the bereaved person make a collage of these photographs and display the collage at the visitation, funeral, or memorial

service. If the adult with mental retardation wants to keep the collage as a remembrance, you may want to help obtain copies of pictures so that the originals can be returned to other family members and friends who loaned them.

9. *Encourage (but do not force) the person to attend the visitation or wake* (**Religious/Spiritual; Ritual/Tradition**). Explain the purpose of this ritual in advance. Be very specific as you discuss what to expect. Provide details. If the casket will be open, describe how the body will look, and that he or she cannot move, open the eyes, or talk. In some traditions, the lower half of the body is covered; describe that the legs are covered, not missing. Explain that mourners may be crying, telling stories about the person who died, hugging each other, and saying, "I'm sorry." Use books, movies, and pictures to help prepare the person in advance. An art therapist reported that she frequently uses a felt board and cutouts she has made to help the person understand what to expect. She has made cutouts to represent various people, the coffin, the body, flowers, the hearse, and so forth.

10. *Encourage (but do not force) the person to attend a funeral or a memorial service* (**Religious/Spiritual; Support from Others; Ritual/Tradition**). Prepare the adult with mental retardation in advance. Explain the purpose of a funeral or memorial service. Describe what will occur during the service and afterward.

11. *Encourage (but do not force) the individual to go to the cemetery for the committal service if a burial plot is utilized* (**Religious/ Spiritual; Ritual/Tradition**). Explain the purpose of this ritual and what will occur. Some families and friends participate in symbolic ways. Some individuals who were close to the deceased place a flower on the grave site or choose a flower from the funeral floral arrangement to take home. Others place a shovel of dirt into the grave.

12. *Videotape or audiotape a funeral or memorial service* (**Spiritual/Religious; Ritual/Tradition; Support from Others; Verbal**).

If the person with mental retardation is unable to attend the funeral or memorial service, consider videotaping or audiotaping it. The authors believe that attending the service in person is most beneficial for the person. There may be extenuating circumstances, however, in which the person with mental retardation is unable to attend the service (for example, if he or she were ill or in the hospital or if the service was held across the country and the person was unable to travel). Discretion should be used in taping the service, and members of the family and the clergy should agree to this process in advance. If the service is taped, please use care when the person views or listens to it. Explain in advance that you have the tape, set up a time to view or listen to it with him or her, allow the person to express emotion as it plays, provide support, and answer questions. Make yourself available or identify someone else who can provide follow-up support for any delayed reactions.

13. *Allow and encourage the person to participate in thanking family and friends for their support* (**Ritual/Tradition**). Following the funeral or memorial service, ask the adult with mental retardation if he or she would like to help write thank-you notes or address envelopes. If he or she is unable to write the notes, encourage the person to sign his or her name to notes written by someone else.

14. *Plan an informal memorial session* (**Ritual/Tradition; Support from Others**). This technique might be particularly helpful if a staff member or peer dies and there are several adults with mental retardation who are grieving. Staff from a group home in Madison, Wisconsin, reported that participants seemed to experience a sense of peace and closure after they hosted an informal memorial session in honor of a young woman, age 35, with mental retardation who had died very unexpectedly. The get-together was conducted a week after the formal church service. The woman's friends, family, and support staff were invited to come to a celebration of her life. They were asked to bring a story about the woman that they could share with the others. The celebration was held in the group home. They played her favorite music in the background. On the dining

room table, they displayed a picture of the woman, a lit candle, items representing her favorite activities, and her favorite beverages. A statement was made by the hostess that they had come together to remember the woman with stories. Then, for one and one-half hours, everyone shared stories that included their interactions with the deceased woman. Refreshments, including the woman's favorite dessert, were served.

15. *Help the person maintain his or her usual routine* (**Support from Others**). To the extent possible, it is a good idea to minimize changes and losses immediately following the death of a loved one. Frequently children and some adults cope with crises by keeping other aspects of their lives the same. It is a way to feel safe and sane in a world that to them has gone awry. Recognize the person's possible need for continuity. Check this assumption with him or her. For example, ask the person if he or she wants to go to work or would rather stay at home. The person may decide to go to work, go shopping with friends, or go to exercise class if these are usual activities. He or she may especially need assistance if the person who died helped him or her do these activities. Help others understand that the person is not showing disrespect by engaging in a usual activity immediately following the death. Similarly, his or her actions should not be interpreted to mean that he or she does not understand death or has recovered already from the loss. Instead, this may be the person's way of coping.

16. *Use bubbles to demonstrate the nature of death* (**Instruct/Teach/Model; Religious/Spiritual**). Use this activity with someone who believes in life after death or to help someone get in touch with memories. Buy a bottle of children's bubble mixture. Blow some bubbles. Catch one. Ask the person if he or she can see the bubble. Ask the person to put his or her hand underneath the bubble and pop it. Ask if he or she can see the bubble any longer. When the person acknowledges that the bubble can no longer be seen, ask if he or she can feel it. It will feel wet on the person's hand. Help him or her understand that this is like someone's death. We no longer can see

the deceased person, and this individual is not with us like before, yet we can remember the deceased person and "feel" him or her in our hearts.

17. *Utilize the concept of a heart beating or assistive technology to help teach someone with severe or profound mental retardation about death* (**Instruct/Teach/Model**). The greater the cognitive disability that someone has (e.g., mental retardation in the severe or profound range rather than mild or moderate), the more difficult it likely will be to teach the person about an abstract concept such as death. There is a greater likelihood that the person will understand the concept as it happens (i.e., at the time of the death of the significant other) and if multiple means are used to explain or demonstrate the concept over time. Thus, it would be helpful to use concrete examples to demonstrate as well as words to describe death. A chaplain has reported that she has been able to help people with severe disabilities understand this concept by teaching them about heartbeats. They can put their hands over their own hearts and feel the beat, they can feel someone else's heart beat, and they can feel that inanimate objects do not have a heartbeat. There are a number of devices on the market that also could be utilized in teaching the concept. A person will feel a sensation if he or she touches a device such as a touch sensor. Thus, the person might get a sense of "alive" by touching the sensor. There are other devices that do something if a person touches a particular key (e.g., a bird will squawk, music will play, and so forth). Someone may be able to get a sense of "alive" by touching the key when the device has a working battery or is connected to electricity and "dead" when nothing happens when he or she touches the key when the battery is removed or the device is not plugged in. An occupational therapist may be a good resource for helping locate devices that could be used for this purpose.

Task II. To Experience the Pain of Grief (See Figure 4.3.)

18. *"Be there" for the person with mental retardation* (**Support from Others**). A 35-year-old woman with mental retardation, whose

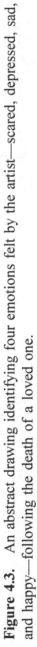

Figure 4.3. An abstract drawing identifying four emotions felt by the artist—scared, depressed, sad, and happy—following the death of a loved one.

father died several years ago, advises the following, "Go over there and cry with them. You give them your best wishes and you try to be helpful to them. . . . You're there if someone wants to lean on your shoulder and cry . . . let it all out. If they want to talk about it, they can talk about it, and if they don't want to talk about it, you can't force them."

Ways to "be there" for someone w.th more severe disabilities are similar. If you do not know the person well, try to build a stable relationship over time so that the person with mental retardation feels familiar and comfortable with you. Sit close to the person when you spend time together. Sit face-to-face rather than side-by-side. Touch the person in a noncompromising location (such as his or her arm) if it is not uncomfortable for him or her. If the person is in a wheel-chair and unable to raise his or her head, get on your knees so that you can see the person's face. If you are walking with someone in a wheelchair, do not always walk behind the chair; try to walk beside the person, or stop frequently to establish eye contact as you talk.

19. *"Join" the person so that he or she does not feel alone* **(Instruct/Teach/Model; Support from Others).** This may be particularly helpful very early in the grief process. Ask the person to make a sound that will tell you how he or she feels. You may need to demonstrate. The sound might be a groan, a moan, a cry, a sigh, etc. After the person makes the unique sound, mimic this sound back to the individual. Encourage the person to do this several times. This exercise will encourage the person to vocalize feelings and help him or her feel support. If the person is nonverbal and uses few sounds, you may be able to demonstrate that you are "joining" him or her by repeating hand movements that the person makes. For example, you may observe that he or she waves his or her hands in the air in a certain pattern. You might try the same behavior, and watch the person's reaction.

20. *If you are grieving also, allow the person to see your grief and talk about it* **(Instruct/Teach/Model; Support from Others;**

Verbal). If you are grief-stricken, at times you will be thinking, speaking, and acting differently than you usually do.

- The person needs to know that he or she is not the cause of your unusual behavior.
- The individual can learn a lot about normal human emotions and about appropriate expression of these emotions by seeing the emotions that you experience and how you handle them. As adults with mental retardation grow older, it is important for them to learn that sadness and crying are "normal" for all adults when a loss has occurred and that they do not have to "hide" their feelings.
- The individual will learn that others feel differently than usual also.
- People feel good when they can help each other. Allow the adult with mental retardation to be part of this give-and-take process and to help you and others during this difficult time. There are many things with which he or she might be able to assist, for example, bringing someone tissues or a beverage, offering a pat on the shoulder, or assisting with child care.

21. *Use books that will assist you to explain the concept of death and the accompanying emotions that someone is likely to experience* **(Instruct/Teach/Model).** Appropriate books can be purchased or borrowed from the library or a hospice near you. Hospices and therapists specializing in grief frequently have bibliographies of recommended books. Choose books that are easy to understand and that have pictures. Some books developed to help children with their grief may be best, but take care to choose books that are not too childish or the grieving adult may feel insulted. If the adult with mental retardation notes that it is a children's book, you can indicate that is true but that many adults have found the book helpful also. You may want to try several books, since reactions will vary from person to person. Following are some books to consider:

- *When Someone Very Special Dies: Children Can Learn to Cope with Grief,* by Marge Heegaard, published in 1988 by

Woodland Press, 99 Woodland Circle, Minneapolis, MN 55424. Phone: (612) 926-2665. This book uses a workbook format and encourages bereaved persons to use drawings to express their feelings. It is designed to be used with a helper over several weeks.

- *Waving Good-Bye: An Activities Manual for Children in Grief*, published in 1990 by The Dougy Center, 3909 S.E. 52nd Avenue, Portland, OR 97206.
- *Saying Goodbye*, by Jim and Joan Boulden, published in 1992 by Boul-den Publishing, P.O. Box 1186, Weaverville, CA 96093.

22. *Use a visual aid to help the person identify how he or she is feeling* (**Instruct/Teach/Model; Support**). Sometimes adults with mental retardation have difficulty expressing their emotions in words or are reluctant to share what they think is a negative emotion. This frequently results in people saying that they are fine or happy or that they are not upset when it is far from the truth. One way to help sort out true emotions is to present options in a nonthreatening, matter-of-fact manner using a concrete visual aide. A visual aide can be drawings or pictures cut from magazines that depict a range of emotions: happy, sad, angry, frightened, and so forth.

One simple technique that has been used very successfully at the Waisman Center Program on Aging & Developmental Disabilities, Madison, Wisconsin, is a page containing simple line drawings of five faces (variations on the much-used smiley face). The five faces depict someone who is very unhappy, somewhat unhappy, neutral, somewhat happy, and very happy. An example is shown in Figure 4.4. The person can be asked which face is most like him or her. "Which one is you? How do you feel today?" "How do you feel about going back to work today?" "How do you feel when you think about the person who died?"

If someone is unaccustomed to sharing his or her feelings, it might be more comfortable to talk first about how others might feel in a similar situation. You might ask, "How do you think someone might feel when his or her mom dies? Do you think that he or she would

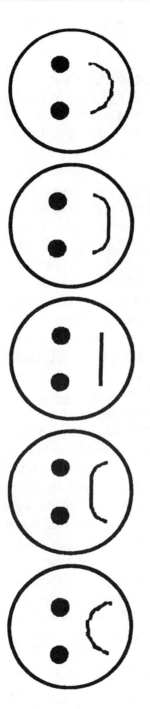

Figure 4.4. An example of a visual aid to help someone communicate how he or she is feeling—very unhappy, somewhat unhappy, neutral, somewhat happy, and very happy.

want to go to the funeral?" Then you can move on to the personal questions about the individual.

23. *Watch the person's reactions closely or enlist the help of others who know him or her well to help you identify the person's feelings* (**Support from Others**). This is especially important as you begin to work with people who are nonverbal or who are unable to share their feelings. Observe the person's body language and sounds. Does he or she convey a negative or positive sense? Identify the person's reactions when happy, when unhappy, when frightened, when confused, etc. Find out what is exciting to the person and how he or she shows that excitement. For example, does the person seem to like the feel of the sun's rays? If so, what behavior tells you this? How does he or she react to a kitten? How does the person react to certain kinds of music? Have you observed a behavior that is unclear to you, but you see the reaction consistently (e.g., turning the head to the right or lifting one foot in the air)? Try to check out the meaning of this behavior with others. You may be able to understand how the individual feels by learning behavior patterns that have been established already.

24. *Acknowledge and affirm the person's feelings* (**Support from Others; Verbal**). A bereaved individual may have a variety of emotions: sadness, anger, fear, confusion, loneliness, or relief. If he or she shares these emotions with you, accept and acknowledge that they are true for him or her. Avoid telling the person how to feel. For example, do not say, "You should be happy that the deceased is no longer suffering." Instead, accept how the bereaved person is feeling and let him or her know that you understand. "Of course you're angry; it's very hard to lose someone you love so much." "Yes, it must be very scary right now, because you lived with your mom your whole life." "Yes, many people cry a lot when someone close to them dies, and you loved your father very much." If the person does not tell you how he or she feels but you observe it, you may want to verify your observations. "You seem to feel grumpy in the morning. Do you miss your mom in the morning? Many people find that mornings are difficult."

25. *Allow and encourage appropriate expression of anger if the person is angry about the death* (**Instruct/Teach/Model; Support from Others; Verbal**). It is important if someone is feeling anger related to a death to express it. Sometimes people have a need to express anger through behavior, rather than just through words. It is never acceptable to injure oneself or others or to damage property. Steer the person to appropriate behaviors, and teach acceptable places and times to express this anger. It may be a good idea to notify others who interact with the bereaved on a regular basis about this anger facilitation, so that they will not misinterpret the person's actions. Some options to consider include engaging in a sport in which a vigorous workout can be obtained (e.g., walking, jogging, swimming, shooting "hoops"); throwing marshmallows or a nerf ball; beating a pillow; screaming in the shower or when no one else is around; smashing ice cubes with a hammer; shredding paper; and pulling weeds. (The latter two would be appropriate if the person can accept direction regarding when these are acceptable and when they are not. For example, what paper can be shredded and what is valuable? Which plants are weeds and which are flowers or vegetables?)

26. *Encourage the bereaved person to draw a picture of himself or herself depicting how he or she is feeling* (**Creative Arts; Support from Others; Verbal**). Provide a variety of colored pencils, markers, crayons, or paints. Encourage the person to draw or paint a picture of himself or herself that will show how he or she is feeling. Encourage the person to explain it to you rather than interpreting it yourself. Try to comment in a neutral way on aspects of the picture rather than praising certain aspects. This will help avoid a situation where the person will draw content to please you. For example, you might comment, "I see that the person in the picture is smiling." Try not to say, "I'm *glad* that the person is smiling." On a future occasion, the person might paint a smiling face in order to please you, even though on that particular day, he or she feels like painting someone who is crying or angry.

If someone has difficulty drawing a picture that depicts his or her feelings, you can ask the person to imagine how someone else might feel in a similar circumstance. "Can you draw a picture of how a man or woman might feel after one of his or her parents has died?" You can later ask if he or she feels like the person in the picture.

One resource to consider is *Ed Emberley's Great Thumbprint Drawing Book*, by Ed Emberley, published in Boston by Little, Brown and Co. in 1977. This book teaches people to draw in a very simple manner using an ink pad and the person's thumbprint as the basis of the drawing. The book contains a section on drawing faces that express different feelings. Since each person has an individual thumbprint, the helper can use this as a symbol to talk with the bereaved about his or her unique feelings. The bereaved also could make fingerprints of all the fingers on his or her hand and give each one a different face. This could be used to help explain to the person that sometimes we feel several different emotions at the same time. For example, he or she may be scared, angry, sad, and happy about some things all at the same time.

27. *Use a slogan to help the person cope* (**Instruct/Teach/ Model; Support from Others**). During the initial stages of grief, the person could be encouraged to use a phrase or slogan to help cope. The process of repeating this phrase when he or she feels particularly upset may help him feel more calm and trigger a sense of being supported. The phrase could be something such as, "I accept" or "I can do this" or "I will be O.K."

28. *Teach the person to chant a phrase or slogan to help cope* (**Instruct/Teach/Model; Music; Support from Others**). Help the person choose a phrase or slogan that will help him or her cope. (See menu item #27.) Ask the person to sing it for you. Chant it back to him or her using the same tones that he or she used. Teach the person appropriate times and locations in which to do this chanting.

29. *Utilize "Spinoza," a teddy bear that plays musical tapes* **(Music).** Someone may find the combination of the music and the cuddliness of the bear to be comforting. You may want to exercise caution in using this teddy bear, since some people do not consider it age-appropriate for adults. It may provide comfort, however, for someone who is not responding to other helping interventions or for someone who has lower cognitive abilities. Hospice organizations and stores providing educational toys may be good sources to locate "Spinoza."

30. *Draw or provide a "body map"* **(Creative Arts).** Ask the person to lie on the floor on top of a large piece of blank newsprint or stand against newsprint that has been taped to the wall. Use a pen or marker to draw a life-size outline of his or her body. (You also could use a small outline of a body that you have drawn or located elsewhere. The book, *When Someone Very Special Dies: Children Can Learn to Cope with Grief* (Heegaard, 1988), contains a body map exercise. (See menu item #21). If you plan to trace the person's body, it is very important to ask permission to do so first; some people can be uncomfortable and view this as an invasion of their personal space. Let the person trace himself or herself between the legs and any other place where he or she may feel sensitive.

Give the person crayons, colored pencils, or markers. Ask the individual to "color" the body map so it looks like how he or she feels inside. Ask the person to describe why certain colors were used and why certain areas of the body were colored differently. Try to avoid giving your own interpretations. You may want to ask the person to do this exercise two or three times over the next year or two. Keep the initial drawings and ask the bereaved individual if he or she can see a change in the pictures.

You also may want to ask the person to color the body map on both sides. (Select heavy paper if the person will be using both sides). On one side the person could draw himself or herself as seen by others, and on the other side the individual could show the feelings that he or she frequently keeps inside.

31. *Identify a prayer, poem, scripture selection, or hymn whose words might bring comfort and meaning to the bereaved individual* (**Religious/Spiritual; Support from Others**). Read it out loud with the bereaved individual, and make a copy of it for him or her if the person can read. A staff member from an agency providing residential support services for adults with developmental disabilities reported that she helped a bereaved individual make a wooden plaque on which were written the words to a comforting poem. The bereaved individual was able to hang the plaque in her home, to take it down and read it, and to carry it with her. See Figures 4.5, 4.6, 4.7, 4.8, and 4.9 for some ideas of prayers, poems, and scripture verses that might be used.

32. *Invite the person to draw or paint a picture that reminds him or her of the person who died* (**Creative Arts; Support from Others**). Provide paints, felt-tip markers, colored pencils, and paper. After the picture is completed, ask the person if he or she would like to talk to you about it. You might obtain clues as to how he or she is feeling by the content of the picture. Do not force your own interpretations of the picture on the person; instead ask for the individual's interpretations. Reflect back to the person some observations about the picture. For example, if a picture of someone crying has been drawn, you might ask if he or she feels like crying. If someone draws a picture of a cemetery, ask if he or she is thinking about the person who was buried at the cemetery; ask if the bereaved person wants to visit the cemetery. If someone enjoys this form of expression, then he or she may want to meet with you several times to create pictures and discuss them.

33. *Offer to pray with the person who is bereaved* (**Religious/ Spiritual; Support from Others**). If the person has religious beliefs that include prayer and you feel comfortable doing so, offer to spend some time with him or her in prayer. Choose a quiet spot where you can be alone. Encourage the person to use his or her own words to pray. If the person has difficulty with this, you may want to offer a simple prayer. For example, "Dear God, thank you so

To my dearest family, some things I'd like to say,
First of all, to let you know, that I arrived okay.
I am writing this from heaven where I dwell with God above
Where there's no more tears of sadness, there is just eternal
love.
Please don't be unhappy just because I'm out of sight,
Remember that I am with you every morning, noon, and night.
That day I had to leave you, when my life on earth was through,
God picked me up and hugged me and He said "I welcome
you.
It's good to have you back again, you were missed while you
were gone,
As for your dearest family, they will be here later on.
I need you here so badly as part of my big plan,
There's so much that we have to do to help our mortal man."
Then God gave me a list of things he wished for me to do,
And most of that list of mine is to watch and care for you.
And I will be beside you every day and week and year,
And when you're sad, I am standing there to wipe away the
tear.
And when you lie in bed at night, the day's chores put to flight,
God and I are closest to you in the middle of the night.
When I think of my life on earth and all those loving years,
Because you're only human, they are bound to bring you tears.
Please do not be afraid to cry, it does relieve the pain,
Remember there would be no flowers unless there was some
rain.
I wish that I could tell you all that God has planned,
But if I were to tell you, you wouldn't understand.
But one thing is for certain, though my life on earth is over,
I am closer to you now than I ever was before.
And to my very many friends, trust God knows what is best.
I'm still not far away from you, I'm just beyond the crest.

(Continued on next page)

There are rocky roads ahead of you and many hills to climb,
But together we can do it taking one day at a time.
It was always my philosophy and I'd like it for you, too,
That as you give unto the world, so the world will give to you.
If you can help somebody who's in sorrow or in pain,
Then you can say to God at night, "My day was not in vain.
And now I am contented that my life, it was worthwhile,
Knowing as I passed along the way, I made somebody smile."
So if you meet somebody who is down and feeling low,
Just lend a hand to pick him up as on your way you go.
When you are walking down the street and you've got me on
    your mind,
I am walking in your footsteps only half a step behind.
And when you feel that gentle breeze or the wind upon your
    face,
That's me giving you a great big hug or just a soft embrace.
And when it's time for you to go from that body to be free,
Remember you are not going, you are coming here to me.
And I will always love you from that land up above,
We'll be in touch again soon. P.S., God sends His love.

—Author Unknown

Figure 4.5.   Sample of a poem that may be comforting to a bereaved person.

THE LORD'S PRAYER
(from *The Small Catechism* by Martin Luther,
in contemporary English)

Our Father, who art in heaven,
Hallowed be thy name.
Thy kingdom come.
Thy will be done
On earth as it is in heaven.
Give us this day our daily bread.
And forgive us our trespasses,
As we forgive those who trespass against us.
And lead us not into temptation,
But deliver us from evil.
For thine is the kingdom,
And the power and the glory forever and ever. Amen

Figure 4.6.   An example of a well-known prayer that may be comforting to a bereaved person.

PSALM 23
(Revised Standard Version)

The Lord is my shepherd, I shall not want;
he makes me lie down in green pastures.
He leads me beside still waters; he restores my soul.
He leads me in paths of righteousness for his name's sake.

Even though I walk through the valley of the shadow of death,
I fear no evil; for thou art with me;
thy rod and thy staff, they comfort me.

Thou preparest a table before me in the presence of my enemies;
thou anointest my head with oil, my cup overflows.
Surely goodness and mercy shall follow me all the days of my
      life;
and I shall dwell in the house of the Lord for ever.

Figure 4.7. Words to Psalm 23 that may be comforting to a bereaved person.

SERENITY PRAYER

God grant me the
serenity to accept the things I cannot change,
courage to change the things I can,
and wisdom to know the difference.

—Author Unknown

Figure 4.8. An example of a well-known short prayer that may be
comforting to a bereaved person.

YISKOR ("Jewish Remembrance")

We Remember Them

In the rising of the sun and in its going down,
we remember them;

In the blowing of the wind and in the chill of winter,
we remember them;

In the warmth of the sun and the peace of summer,
we remember them;

In the rustling of the leaves and the beauty of autumn,
we remember them;

In the beginning of the year and when it ends,
we remember them;

When we are weary and in need of strength,
we remember them;

When we are lost and sick at heart,
we remember them;

When we have joys we yearn to share,
we remember them;

So long as we live, they too shall live,
for they are now a part of us,
as we remember them.

Figure 4.9. Copy of the *Yiskor,* a Jewish prayer of remembrance, which may be comforting to bereaved persons of any ethnic or religious background.

much for giving me such a wonderful mom. I love her very much. I miss her, but I am glad that she does not hurt and that she is safe with you. Please be with me and help me feel better. Amen." You also might include prayers that have been a part of his or her religious tradition, for example, the Lord's Prayer (Figure 4.6), Psalm 23 (Figure 4.7), the Serenity Prayer (Figure 4.8), or the Yiskor (Figure 4.9). It is important to be aware of your own religious viewpoints and to take care not to force these upon the grieving person.

34. *Help the person purchase or compile an audiotape of favorite hymns* (**Music; Religious/Spiritual**). Investigate the person's religious background if you are unfamiliar with it. If he or she is someone who derives comfort from music, identify some hymns that are comforting to the person. You can do this by asking the individual the names of his or her favorite hymns; seeing if he or she can sing some to you; speaking with the family about hymns that might be part of the person's religious heritage; speaking with a clergy member, church music director, or choir director about music that many parishioners find comforting; or playing a number of hymns and having the person identify which he or she likes best. Purchase or make a special audiotape of this music that the person can play when he or she would like this type of comfort.

35. *Help the person create a "feelings box"* (**Creative Arts**). This activity helps distinguish between those feelings that a person may be showing to the outside world (e.g., "I'm fine.") versus those that he or she may be feeling on the inside (e.g., "I'm sad, lonely, scared, or angry."). It is helpful to have a variety of differently sized small boxes (shoe box size or smaller), a sizable number of pictures cut from magazines or a stack of magazines, markers with which to write, and glue. The person then can make a box collage. The individual can choose a box and glue pictures on the outside of the box that show the face that he or she shows to others; inside the box, the person can put pictures, drawings, or words of how he or she really feels. Other material can be added to the box as well, including such items as fabric, ribbon, yarn, cotton, or tissue paper. People may

find meaning in using items that are certain colors or textures. For example, some individuals have used cotton to cushion the inside of their box, placing cut-out hearts or other meaningful pictures into the cotton.

Some people may want to decorate only the inside of the box initially and gradually decorate the outside. This may help them identify and accept initial feelings of grief. Then slowly they incorporate changes in how they feel and consequently in the feelings that they reveal to others. If the box has a cover, the person may feel less vulnerable and choose to maintain privacy by leaving the box closed. He or she can be encouraged to share his or her feelings by keeping the lid open more and more. The person may want to change the pictures or create a new box as time goes on.

36. *Find a comforting place to relax near water* (**Nature/ Outdoors**). Often sitting or being near a lake, pond, stream, river, marsh, or ocean can be soothing. Water is an essential element for life; reconnecting to it in nature can help someone regain a sense of the natural flow of life and death. Spending time near water often releases someone's inner thoughts and feelings. It is almost as if someone were dipping below the surface to release what is in his or her mind and heart. This can help unburden the grief that the person may be carrying.

37. *Go out on water* (**Nature/Outdoors**). This is an activity for people who are not afraid of a body of water. Choose a day when the water is relatively calm. The activity of going out on the water in a boat or floating on an air mattress in the water and feeling the ebb and flow of the water can be soothing. Some communities have a special pontoon boat for people with disabilities. Fees often are reduced. Check with your community recreation program to see if a boat is available in your community.

38. *Release a message on the water* (**Nature/Outdoors; Ritual/ Tradition**). Whether someone is sitting by water or is on the water,

he or she may want to consider releasing tiny notes with personal thoughts, feelings, or memories on them. These thoughts and feelings may be written, or they may be in the form of a picture or doodle that represents the idea or emotion that he or she would like to release. The activity of throwing notes into the water and watching them drift away can help lighten some of the emotional turmoil that is felt after the death of a loved one. If you choose to try this menu item, the authors request that the impact on the environment be considered. Balance the potential benefit of doing this exercise with the impact it will make on the environment.

39. _Bury a message or note_ **(Nature/Outdoors; Physical; Ritual/ Tradition).** The message or note may be about something that has been hard to let go—perhaps a difficult memory or issue about the person who has died or a regret. This act is called a ritual. The ritual does not erase the memory but may help the person recognize the importance of "letting go" of the energy and emotion that is still going into it. The note may be written ahead of time, or the person may want to take paper and pen, find a pleasant spot outdoors, and write the note there. Remember to bring a garden trowel or small shovel to use to bury the note. It is recommended that this activity be done on private property. Please try to leave the land as you found it.

40. _Light four symbolic candles and discuss their meaning_ **(Music; Ritual/Tradition).** Light four candles and label each with one of the following words: grief, courage, memory, and love. Talk briefly about the meaning of these words. Give the bereaved an unlit candle. Encourage the person to light his or her candle from the others. He or she can light it from one, several, or all four. Encourage the person to discuss why the particular candle(s) was chosen to light his or her own. If safety issues or building regulations do not allow the use of candles, you might use flashlights and revise the ritual accordingly. For example, rather than lighting the candle from others, the bereaved person could touch his or her flashlight to others. You will find a candle-lighting ceremony shown in Figure 4.10. You also may want to use music to enhance this ritual. Paul Alexander has

As we light these four candles in honor of you, we light one for our grief, one for our courage, one for our memories, and one for our love.

Light the first candle. This candle represents our grief. The pain of losing you is intense. It reminds us of the depth of our love for you.

Light the second candle. This candle represents our courage—to confront our sorrow—to comfort each other —to change our lives.

Light the third candle. This light is in your memory— the times we laughed, the times we cried—the times we were angry with each other—the silly things you did—the caring and joy you gave us.

Light the fourth candle. This light is the light of love. As we enter this holiday season, day by day we cherish the special place in our hearts that will always be reserved for you. We thank you for the gift your living brought to each of us. We love you.

Figure 4.10. Candle ritual developed by Paul Alexander.

composed a song, *Light a Candle,* to accompany this ritual. Tapes are available from Paul Alexander Music, P.O. Box 125, Rockville Center, NY 11571.

41. *Use rocks and helium balloons to demonstrate relief after sharing feelings* **(Instruct/Teach/Model; Ritual/Tradition).** Collect small rocks and label each with a difficult feeling such as angry, sad, and jealous. Put them in a basket and attach a sufficient number of helium balloons so that when the rocks are removed, the balloons lift the basket. Ask the person to help you remove the rocks labeled with the difficult emotions. Encourage him or her to talk about these emotions in relation to the loss that has been experienced. Demonstrate that over time, as people share their emotions, they no longer will be "weighted down" and they will feel better again.

42. *Walk in an enjoyable location while you talk with the person about how he or she is coping* **(Nature/Outdoors; Physical; Support from Others; Verbal).** Sometimes it can be difficult to share thoughts and emotions while sitting in a room. Emotions can feel too intense or the person can feel singled out in a negative way. Consider walking with the person in an enjoyable location. You still can find private space, and the activity of walking can make it easier to talk. As you walk, gently urge the individual to talk about his or her feelings or about the person who died. Do not be afraid of silence; during quiet times the person may be gathering his or her thoughts or simply finding comfort in the activity and your presence.

43. *Help the person live "one day at a time," planning especially for times of the day that might be particularly difficult* **(Instruct/Teach/Model; Support from Others).** If the bereaved had lived with the person who died or had received support and companionship from this person on a regular basis, life may seem very frightening and/or lonely without this support and companionship. Help the person understand that on some days he or she may feel very sad or angry and on other days will feel O.K. Help him or her

write out the plans or schedule for the day. For example: Will he or she go to work? What time will he or she leave for work? What time will he or she return home? What will the individual do after work and after dinner? Times of the day, week, or month that were spent with the person who died may be particularly difficult times. Help the person determine the best ways to spend these times. Does he or she want to be left alone to grieve or would it be helpful to plan to go to another location, be with someone else, or try something new?

44. _Encourage the person to design a greeting card_ **(Creative Arts).** Most people send and/or receive greeting cards for many purposes. Many have felt comfort, support, and friendship when they have received cards. This activity will enable the person to have a card that meets his or her exact needs, since the person will be creating it. A variety of materials, colors, pictures, and designs that the person finds pleasing and soothing can be used. Encourage the person to write in it what he or she would like to hear.

The card also could be designed for someone else, including the deceased person. In the latter situation, the activity could be described in the following manner, "If it were possible for _____ to see and read this card, what would you like to tell him or her in pictures and words?"

45. _Help the person make a tape or series of tapes of music for the deceased person to "hear"_ **(Music).** Some people have not had a chance to say good-bye or to tell the deceased person something from the heart. Music is one way to help the person express thoughts and feelings. Music may express ideas or emotions that have been or continue to be difficult for the person to say aloud. Encourage the person to choose music that he or she would like the deceased person to hear if it were possible.

46. _Help the person make a tape of music to help cope and move on with life_ **(Music).** Music may nurture and help heal the

person. Assist the bereaved in identifying music that he or she personally finds encouraging and uplifting. Suggest that this special tape be played when he or she engages in daily activities around home.

47. *Help the individual compile a relaxation tape using recordings of instrumental music* **(Music).** Identify someone who is familiar with progressive relaxation and who would be willing to help record a tape. (This might be a social worker, music therapist, or psychologist. People who have led stress management groups will be especially familiar with relaxation techniques.) Help the person choose soothing, relaxing, instrumental music. On one side of the tape, record instructions for progressive relaxation utilizing the selected music as background sound. On the other side of the tape, record only the music. Practice with the person, teaching him or her how to listen to the tape and relax. In time, the person may choose to use only the musical side. The tape can be used daily to help the person develop a sense of peace and calmness or as a sleep aide.

48. *Identify a music therapist with whom the person could work* **(Music; Support from Others).** A music therapist could assist the person with grief work using the medium of music. There are approximately 3,500 registered music therapists in the country. Please see chapter 5, "Professional Assistance," for information on how to locate a music therapist in your area.

49. *Help the person get in touch with his or her feelings about the death by having a discussion based on the following or similar statements* **(Support from Others; Verbal).**

- Sometimes I wish that . . .
- When I'm alone . . .
- If I could change anything, I would . . .
- The thing that I miss most about my loved one is . . .
- I'm happy that . . .
- I look forward to the future because . . .

50. *Touch base at regular intervals with the bereaved person about the death* (**Support from Others; Verbal**). In general, people frequently do not talk about a death or how they are coping after the funeral or memorial service occurs. Yet they may well be having a difficult time and could be helped by the support of others. Some adults with mental retardation seem to understand these cultural norms and do not want to upset someone else by bringing up the subject of death. If the person is someone who does not speak about the death, it is a good idea to touch base with him or her at regular intervals about the death and about how he or she is coping. Use your discretion about the appropriate span of time (e.g., every month or every other month). One way to initiate the topic is to say, "I was thinking about _____ (the deceased person) the other day. Do you ever think about_____? What do you think about?" By doing this, you may be able to prevent complicated grief reactions from occurring or to identify problems early and help the person obtain professional help if needed.

Task III. To Adjust to an Environment in Which the Deceased Is Missing (See Figure 4.11.)

51. *"Finger dance" to connect with someone* (**Music; Support from Others**). If you begin to work with someone who is nonverbal or who has difficulty verbalizing, you may want to "finger dance" with that person as a way to establish rapport. Put your hand in the air and ask the person to put his or her hand against yours. Move your hands and fingers in different ways to simulate dancing. For example, you can move your fingers against each other in time to music. Motion can include small movements with fingers only or larger movements involving the arms. Thumbs can be interlocked and "twirl." You can vary the pressure of your hands against each other. Encourage him or her to initiate hand movements. You may want to play music as you "dance."

52. *Encourage dancing to express feeling* (**Music; Physical**). This activity may be especially helpful for someone who is nonver-

Figure 4.11. A grieving person and her deceased sister—who is an angel now—and what helps the grieving person the most—her church.

bal or who has more severe cognitive impairment. You might talk briefly about the person who died and then play different types of music and encourage the bereaved person to move or dance to the music according to how he or she feels.

53. *Enlarge and frame a meaningful photo* (**Creative Arts; Ritual/Tradition**). A 48-year-old man with mental retardation reported that he found comfort in placing a photograph of his family of origin in a place in his bedroom where he could see it when he got up in the morning and then again the last thing at night. Both of his parents were deceased and he referred to them frequently as "My dear, sweet mother and dad." He liked to take the picture with him to show to new staff and other people with whom he had occasion to interact. The picture seemed to serve as a visual reminder, that while his parents were no longer alive and his siblings might not be able to be with him often, he was a member of a loving family.

54. *Help the person identify others who will provide support for him* (**Support from Others**). This list would include family members, friends, and staff to whom he can turn for help or support on difficult days. It may be helpful if you make this list visual for the person. It might be a sheet on which are listed helpers and their telephone numbers. It could be a diagram depicting the person with mental retardation in the middle of a page of paper and the names of people to whom he or she can turn for help around the outside of the page with lines drawn toward the middle. Or it might be a picture display including photographs of people who care about the bereaved person.

Additionally, it may be helpful to identify the type of support that people on this list can provide. For example, ask the person with which people he or she could talk when feeling sad, which people would accept an invitation to engage in a leisure activity, and who might attend church with him or her.

55. *Assist the person to attend a grief support group* (**Support from Others**). If the person has verbal abilities, enjoys being a member

of a group, and in general listens when others are talking without repeatedly interrupting, he or she may benefit and contribute to a grief support group for the general public. You can locate support groups in your area by contacting a hospice organization, funeral director, church, or synagogue, or by consulting a local calendar of events.

The person may be more comfortable if you attend the group also. This will help you know what he or she experienced in the group as you continue to provide support. Once there, many people with mental retardation can participate just like any other member of the group, without additional assistance from their support persons. Several leaders of grief support groups have reported that adults with mental retardation have been helpful in the groups. Their honest expression of feelings and questions can "break the ice" for other group members who felt the same way but who were reticent to open up.

56. *Help the bereaved individual obtain an item that belonged to the deceased individual* **(Ritual/Tradition).** Allow the bereaved individual to choose an item that is meaningful to him or her. Several adults with mental retardation have reported that they wanted to have something that previously belonged to the deceased. In each situation, the person was very clear what would be helpful.

- A 61-year-old woman, an only child, wanted a ring that had belonged to her mother.
- A 48-year-old man found comfort sitting in a lounge chair that had been a favorite of his grandfather who had been his primary care provider.
- A 31-year-old woman wanted, as a remembrance, some of the children's books and toys that had been stored in a toy chest at her grandparents' home in anticipation of the visits from grandchildren. She described vivid details of playing with these toys as a child while visiting her grandparents. Having some of them meant a great deal to her.

57. *Enable the person to make a scrapbook of sympathy cards* (**Creative Arts**). The person might purchase an album for this purpose or create one from a variety of art supplies. The album could be a place to paste sympathy cards and letters of condolence that the family received.

58. *Help the person identify "buddies" for support* (**Instruct/ Teach/Model; Support from Others**). Locate one or more people with mental retardation who also have experienced the death of someone close to them. They might be located through a local chapter of an organization such as The Arc (an advocacy agency for people with mental retardation) or a vocational agency. Arrange for the person whom you are supporting to meet these other people. Explore with them the idea of being "buddies" to help each other on days that they are feeling sad, angry, or lonely. Talk to them about the type of support that they could give each other either on the phone or when meeting in person:

- listening when the other person needs to talk about the person who died or about how he or she is feeling,
- offering suggestions to the other person, and
- sharing their experiences and what helps them on bad days.

After a meeting or two, the "buddies" may be able to connect on their own, without someone else helping to facilitate the process.

59. *Look at photo albums together* (**Support from Others**). Reminisce about occasions spent with the deceased. You may want to make duplicate copies of favorite pictures. The bereaved individual could have these to carry in his or her wallet or purse, to place under the pillow at night, to paste in a memory workbook, or to develop a new photo album entitled "Remembering Mom (Dad, or the name of the person who died)."

60. *Help the person obtain rides to the cemetery if he or she would like to visit it* (**Support from Others**). Some people find help in grieving or have a sense of honoring the deceased person if they

are able to visit the grave site either occasionally or on a regular basis. The bereaved may want to place flowers that he or she has picked or chosen on the grave on holidays (e.g., Memorial Day) or other special days such as the birthday of the deceased person, the day the loved one died, Mother's Day, or Father's Day.

61. *Plan periodic memory dinners* **(Ritual/Tradition; Support from Others; Verbal).** Initially designate a day each month when the dinner hour will be used to honor the memory of the person who died. For example, the date might be the first or last day of the month or the date the loved one was born (e.g., the 26th of each month) Prepare a special meal and reminisce about the person who died. Over time, you may want to decrease the frequency of these memory dinners to once or twice a year (for example, the loved one's birth date and the date of death). This type of ritual dinner will help assure the grieving person that the loved one will not be forgotten. You may want to include one of the other rituals described in this booklet at the end of the meal. A special prayer also could be used. One very appropriate prayer is the Jewish prayer of remembrance, the Yiskor (Figure 4.9).

62. *Use candles on anniversary dates as a way to symbolically remember a loved one who has died* **(Ritual/Tradition).** Anniversary dates are frequently difficult for people. An anniversary date can be the birthday of a deceased loved one or the date of death. Sometimes the bereaved individual is not even conscious that an anniversary date is occurring yet shows distress through emotions or behavior.

A group home for women with mental retardation in Madison, Wisconsin, acknowledges that anniversary dates are difficult and helps the women through the day by remembering their loved one. The staff keep a supply of small candles on hand. The women are instructed to bring a candle to the dinner table if that day is an anniversary date for them. During dinner, the candle is lit in remembrance of the person who died. Conversation may include reminiscing about the deceased person. All the residents of the home know that if someone plans to light a candle that night, she may be sad, angry, or upset during the day. The candle helps symbolize that the deceased person is remembered and also is a sign to others who live in the residence that the person may need additional emotional support that day.

63. *Design a memory workbook* (**Creative Arts**). Help the person make a memory workbook about the person who died. The content can vary depending on the individual. Some items to consider include the following:

- a picture of the deceased person,
- a copy of the obituary,
- a copy of the memorial card,
- a list of the deceased person's favorite things (color, activities, food, places to visit),
- a list of what the bereaved person enjoyed doing with the deceased,
- a list of what the bereaved person will miss about the loved one,
- a list of what the bereaved person will NOT miss about the person (To foster a realistic, balanced perspective of the deceased, it is a good idea to include both positive and negative traits of a deceased individual.),
- a "letter" from the bereaved individual telling the deceased person what he or she would like the deceased to know, and
- a "letter" from the deceased person (For example, "If _____ were alive, what would he or she write to you in a letter? What do you think he or she would want to tell you? What would you like to hear him or her say to you?").

The workbook will be helpful to the person at the time he or she is making it as well as in the future. On days when the person is feeling sad, lonely, or vulnerable, the individual can page through it, carry it with him or her, or add to it.

One memory workbook that is already developed and ready to use is *Memory Book for Bereaved Children,* by Kathleen Braza, available from Healing Resources, P. O. Box 9478, Salt Lake City, UT 84109. Phone: (801) 484-8220 or (800) 473-HEAL.

64. *Help the person keep a journal* **(Instruct/Teach/Model; Creative Arts).** Many people in the general population benefit from maintaining a daily diary, log, or journal. A journal can be used to note events that occurred, emotions experienced, or dreams for the future. A live-in residential staff member helped a 30-year-old Wisconsin woman with mental retardation understand the concept of a parent's death and ultimately cope with her father's death through the use of a journal. The staff person did the actual writing, using the woman's words as much as possible. They started the journal by writing, "This is my log book to help me understand how to accept a loss of life, how to live with it, and how to keep surviving and going on with my own life." They recorded facts (e.g., Dad is looking worse today) and feelings (e.g., I'm scared; I don't want to lose him). They discussed and recorded the names of people in her life to whom she could turn for support, the skills she had attained and how independent she had become, and events to look forward to during the upcoming year. The log book was something tangible that the woman could pick up, read, and hold.

65. *Help the person obtain or create a musical tape that includes favorite songs the person enjoyed with the deceased* **(Music).** These might be lullabies or songs that the deceased sang to the bereaved person when he or she was young or favorite songs that they enjoyed together over the years.

66. *Help the person compile a videotape from home videos as a way to remember the deceased* **(Creative Arts).** If the family is one that has enjoyed commemorating family events by taking videos, help the person obtain copies of several of these that have special meaning for him or her. Or help compile a special video in remembrance of the person who died by combining segments of several

home videos. Videos also can be developed using a number of photographs.

67. *Help the person create a memory box* (**Creative Arts**). The box can be large or small. It might be purchased or created by covering a cardboard box with fabric, wallpaper, or gift wrap. A woman with Down syndrome reported that she stored keepsakes in a fishing tackle box, which had belonged to a family member. In the box, a person can place mementos of his or her relationship with the person who died. These mementos can be anything that has meaning for the person—pictures, cards and letters, an article of clothing (e.g., a favorite shirt), jewelry, a watch, a favorite game or objects from a favorite activity (e.g., knitting needles or fishing lures), a copy of the obituary, and sympathy cards. The list is endless. Some people feel comforted by looking through this type of memory box periodically. Seeing and holding objects is a way to help them "connect" with their memories of the deceased person.

68. *Use a symbolic memory bag of rocks* (**Ritual/Tradition; Verbal**). Place a variety of small rocks in a bag. (Using a cloth bag is especially nice.) Include some smooth, polished stones and some that are rough with jagged edges. Ask the person to choose a rock from the bag and, after doing so, to share a memory of the person who died. Do this several times. This is a way to demonstrate that memories are real, that people have more than one memory about someone, and possibly that people have more than one emotion attached to these memories. For example, perhaps in the course of this exercise they have identified memories of happy, sad, silly, and embarrassing events. Using rough stones helps people identify that there may be some memories that are "sharp" and hurt to think about. They also can be helped to understand that by identifying these "sharp" memories and expressing their feelings, the memories can be replaced with "smoother" memories (represented by the polished stones).

69. *Help the person create a bracelet, necklace, or decoration from beads in memory of the person who died* (**Creative Arts;**

Support from Others). First, assist the person in identifying some memories about the deceased. Then encourage the person to select beads that are reminders of these memories. For example, the person might select a white bead for someone's snowy hair, a rough bead for someone's rough hands, or a bead with a symbol on it such as a heart or an initial. There are many different kinds of beads available at bead stores or arts and craft shops. The beads can be strung to form a jewelry item or a colorful strand to hold or display. Encourage the person to wear, carry, or display the item.

70. *Use a collection of sea shells to help the bereaved individual talk about the deceased* **(Ritual/Tradition; Verbal).** Place a collection of sea shells in a box or basket. Ask the person to choose one that reminds him or her in some way of the person who died. Encourage the person to describe why he or she chose this particular shell. Examples of statements you might hear include the following: "I chose this one because it's broken—like my heart." "I chose this one because it is big, and my dad was big." This is a way to encourage someone to talk about the deceased person, and the bereaved person's memories and emotions.

71. *Develop a collection related to the deceased person, and use this collection as a way to reminisce* **(Creative Arts).** The collection should in some way remind the bereaved about the person who died. Ideas for the collection are endless. If the person liked to fish, it might be a collection of fishing lures. If he or she enjoyed sports, it might consist of sports memorabilia. It could be a recipe collection. If the deceased liked cats, it might be a collection of items depicting cats. The collection could contain items that were made by the deceased, cards or letters that the deceased person had sent, or gifts that he or she had given to others. It might be a collection of favorite belongings of the deceased—a watch, jewelry, favorite shirt or sweater, or a favorite book. The person may want to add to this collection over time or keep the collection intact to help reminisce periodically.

72. <u>*Set aside time to talk with the bereaved person about his or her life in the past and compare and contrast it with life currently*</u> (**Support from Others; Verbal**). As a way to help the person adjust to a new life, spend some time talking or writing down some aspects of the person with mental retardation's life prior to the death and what his or her life is like now. Acknowledge the changes that have occurred. Talk about emotions that he or she has felt about the changes. Encourage the person to talk about all types of changes—those that are positive, negative, and neutral.

73. <u>*Help the person compile a musical audiotape that serves as a "scrapbook of musical memories"*</u> (**Music**). A traditional scrapbook holds mementos, cards, letters, and pictures reminding people of events that were important to them. A musical tape that serves as a "musical scrapbook" might contain music that was played at events that the person enjoyed attending with the deceased. For example, it might contain music from athletic events, a circus, or a musical play. Such a tape will help the person remember and reminisce about happy times spent together.

74. <u>*Help the person write a song*</u> (**Music**). A bereaved person who enjoys music may be inclined to write a song or work on a song with someone else who is musically inclined. A piano or a music program on a computer could be used to determine musical notes. (For example, the helper could identify if the bereaved person wanted the music to go "up" [and demonstrate] or "down" [and demonstrate].) They could write down the words that they wanted to use. When completed, the bereaved may want to practice and play or sing it for others to hear.

75. <u>*Create new words to familiar songs*</u> (**Music**). A bereaved person may want to write new words to familiar tunes that express his or her feelings and thoughts related to the death and life now. One way to help the person do this is to choose songs that have a refrain and let the person fill in the blank. For example, the musical phrase, "Sometimes I feel like a motherless child," can be changed

to however the person is feeling—"Sometimes I feel *just too tired to move.*" "Sometimes I feel *both happy and sad.*"

76. <u>*Help the person shop for a special C.D. or musical tape*</u> **(Music).** Identify whether the person would like to listen to an instrumental or vocal recording. Ask what he or she would like the music to do. For example, does the individual want soft, quiet music to help feel calm, or lively music to help escape sadness for a while. Help the bereaved person consider music for the following purposes: to grieve, to heal, or to honor the deceased person.

77. <u>*Help the person contribute money in memory of the deceased*</u> **(Ritual/Tradition).** Help the person utilize money received from memorials to contribute to an organization that was important to the deceased. Examples include musical organizations, schools, environmental organizations, civic clubs, veteran's organizations, churches, or synagogues. Help the person obtain a copy of a program or report in which the donation is acknowledged. If the donation has been given to a performing arts organization, he or she may want to attend a performance.

78. <u>*Help the person form or join a drumming circle*</u> **(Music; Support from Others).** A growing number of people are finding release through drumming circles. These are groups of people who come together for support and utilize drums as a way to communicate their inner feelings. (For example, different drums, drumsticks, rhythms, or loudness will help them communicate their emotions.) To locate a drumming circle or information about one in your area, contact music therapists or psychotherapists.

79. <u>*Assist the person in creating a design on a tee shirt that helps him or her remember the person who has died*</u> **(Creative Arts; Ritual/Tradition).** Any of the following can be used: fabric, fabric paint, fabric crayons, markers. Fabric and craft shops are good places to locate supplies and ideas. Bereaved people frequently recreate designs that depict familiar or favorite memories shared with the deceased person.

80. *Provide flowers for a church service in memory of the person who died* (**Spiritual/Religious; Ritual/Tradition**). Many churches gladly accept small donations to be used for flowers for weekly services and special plants or flowers for holiday services. The bereaved person may want to contribute money to purchase flowers in memory of the person who died. The deceased person's birthday and holidays are good times to do this.

81. *Obtain and watch a video with the bereaved person related to coping with the loss of a loved one* (**Instruct/Teach/Model; Support from Others**). A number of videos have been designed for people who are grieving. A hospice organization is one of the best sources to obtain information about videos for this purpose. Some videos to consider include: *Listen to Your Sadness: Finding Hope Again after Despair Invades Your Life*; *How Do I Go On?: Redesigning Your Future after Crisis Has Changed Your Life*; and *Invincible Summer: Returning to Life after Someone You Love Has Died*. All three are by James E. Miller, Willowgreen Productions, P.O. Box 25180, Ft. Wayne, IN 46825. Phone: (219) 424-7916. Another available video is *Whitewater: The Positive Power of Grief*, produced in association with ACCORD, INC. by AGS Media, 1941 Bishop Lane, Suite 207, Louisville, KY 40218. Phone: (800) 346-3087.

It is a good idea to talk with the bereaved person after viewing a video to identify how he or she is feeling and to clarify any misconceptions that might have been formed.

82. *Obtain and watch a movie with the bereaved person that depicts other people who are coping with losses* (**Instruct/Teach/Model; Support from Others**). Visit a business that rents video movies or purchase a guide to movies out in video format to identify those that have a theme related to coping with a loss. Help the bereaved person choose a movie and watch it with him or her. It is a good idea to discuss the movie after viewing it to determine how the person is feeling and to clarify any misconceptions that might have been

formed. You also might discuss how the movie was similar to the bereaved person's loss and how it was not similar. This activity can help the bereaved person understand that loss is a part of every person's life, and he or she will be able to see other people try to cope with the deaths of loved ones.

83. *Encourage "story-telling" about the person who died* (**Support from Others; Verbal**). Encourage the bereaved person to talk about events from the past that were shared with the deceased person. If you knew the deceased person, share your stories as well. Try to include others who knew the deceased person (e.g., siblings, aunts and uncles, close friends) in the process of story-telling. Stories can be about any event in the past—anecdotes from childhood, later years, holidays, special events, routine daily activities, funny stories, sad stories, happy stories, events surrounding the illness or accident, and the death itself. This story-telling helps the bereaved person come to terms with the loss, feel support from others, build relationships with others, and learn more about the deceased or come to terms with aspects of his or her relationship with the deceased person (Rosenblatt & Elde, 1990).

84. *Ask specific questions to help the bereaved person reminisce about the person who died* (**Support from Others; Verbal**). If someone has difficulty reminiscing about the person who died, you might ask some specific questions to help. If you also knew the deceased person, you can share an anecdote about the person who died and then ask the bereaved person if he or she has another memory to share with you. Topics to consider include the following:

- What was a happy time that you shared with the person?
- What was a funny time?
- What did you like best about the person who died?
- What will you miss most about the person who died?
- What did you not like about the person who died? (It is important to include both positive and negative traits of a deceased individual to foster a realistic, balanced perspective.)

85. *If desired, help the person attend a church or synagogue of his or her choice* **(Spiritual/Religious).** Religious organizations historically have provided support and solace to people in troubling times. Following the death of someone close, a person may want to attend or reconnect with a church or temple. The bereaved individual may want especially for someone to accompany him or her to the services. Realize that poignant prayers, music, or words can cause a person to show emotion unexpectedly (e.g., crying) during the worship service. Some people may want to continue attending church because of the comfort or support that they feel. Others may avoid such a setting because they do not want to show their emotions in public. Allow the bereaved person to choose what is most helpful to him or her.

86. *Plan and participate in an anniversary ritual* **(Ritual/ Tradition).** It should be expected that a person's grief will return on the anniversary of the deceased person's death. Many people find that engaging in some tradition or ritual will give them something concrete to do at this time and provide an opportunity for remembering the loved one.

Some religious traditions (e.g., Catholicism) and some cultural groups (e.g., Muslims, Jews, Buddhists and the Lakota, among others) recognize anniversaries with ceremonies or rituals a year after the loved one's death (Irish, Lundquist, & Jenkins Nelson, 1993; Weizman & Kamm, 1985). People who are Catholic may attend a special mass for the deceased. Families may visit the grave to bring flowers and pray. A special candle may be lit in the church. In Judaism, a candle may be lit at home. A prayer of remembrance may be recited at a synagogue service, and the name of the deceased may be read.

An anniversary ritual can be created no matter what the bereaved person's religious or cultural traditions are. A variety of activities could be done to remember the deceased person at this time. Someone might arrange for a prayer service to focus on the memory of the deceased person. Someone else might look at photographs and spend time with family and friends reminiscing. Perhaps a special meal (e.g., including the favorite foods of the deceased person) will be shared. Special flowers for the table may be purchased. Maybe the bereaved person will want to engage in a favorite hobby or pastime that he or she did with the deceased. Perhaps the person would like to go to a favorite location that had been enjoyed with the deceased, such as a park, store, or sports arena. To the extent possible, the person with mental retardation should be an active participant in determining how best to remember the deceased person.

87. *Use a timeline to help the bereaved person gain a perspective on his or her own life and ability to cope with challenges in the past* (**Creative Arts; Support from Others; Verbal**). Jewett (1982) has described how to utilize time-lines in her book, *Helping Children Cope with Separation and Loss* (pp. 100-103). She discussed the strong impact a technique such as this can have because multiple modalities are used; that is, people can be helped to *see* their lives, *hear* about their lives, and review how they *felt* at different times during their lives.

When events occur that can cause confusion in someone's life, such as a death, it may be helpful to review the person's life with him or her using a timeline as a tool. This can be done in several ways. A line can be drawn on a large piece of newsprint, or a piece of yarn can be strung up in a room. Words and pictures then can be attached to the timeline and a picture of the person's life can be portrayed graphically. Markers on the timeline will be special events in the person's life—birth, moving to new locations, graduation from school, starting and ending jobs, deaths, and new people entering the bereaved person's life. This information can be written on the timeline or attached to it. Photographs, magazine pictures, drawings that the bereaved person creates, newspaper clippings, and the program from a funeral all could be used.

During the process of doing the timeline, the helper will discuss the following with the bereaved person: the event, people involved in the event, and the emotions surrounding the event. For example, the helper might say, "When you were born, your parents were very happy. They might have been a little scared, too, because they had never taken care of a tiny baby before." The helper will encourage the bereaved person to tell his or her own story and to share his or her emotions regarding the various events. For example, "Do you remember how you felt when you started your new job?" "How did you feel last year at the funeral?" The helper may want to use the timeline on more than one occasion with the bereaved individual.

88. *Help the person be more independent; focus on his or her competence and abilities* **(Instruct/Teach/Model; Support From Others).** The bereaved person possibly has more abilities than have been demonstrated by past activities. This may be especially true if the person has lived with his or her parents and the parents simply always have taken care of certain daily living tasks such as washing clothes, grocery shopping, and lawn care. If the bereaved had been living with the person who died, this is an ideal time to assist him or her in learning new skills. Frequent praise may be very helpful. In this way, the bereaved individual not only will have a loss, but also will be gaining a new source of self-esteem. One caution, however, is not to expect the person to be able to learn new skills immediately, particularly those with multiple steps. This is especially true when the bereaved is in need of support during the early stages of grief and may have a decreased ability to concentrate.

89. *Determine how the person is feeling 9 to 12 months and again at 18 months following the death* **(Support from Others).** Do not assume that "no news is good news." If you do not hear the person talking about the deceased, it does not necessarily mean that he or she has recovered. Take the initiative to ask some questions and observe his or her behavior to determine if the person would benefit from continued or additional assistance.

**Task IV. To Withdraw Emotional Energy
and Reinvest It (See Figure 4.12.)**

90. *Plant a tree or other vegetation in honor of the person who
died* **(Nature/Outdoors; Ritual/Tradition).** Explain the purpose of
a memorial to the bereaved individual (i.e., that a memorial is something that we do to remember someone who died). Help the bereaved
choose a tree or other vegetation and plant it and care for it. The
plant can be located indoors or outdoors but should be in a location
to which the bereaved person has access. Allow and encourage the
bereaved individual to choose the vegetation and to provide as much
care for it as he or she is able.

91. *Encourage peer interactions around the subject of death*
(Support from Others; Verbal). The following anecdote is from a
case manager in Michigan. Staff members helped a group of older
persons with developmental disabilities form a group or club, which
would meet on a regular basis. The purpose of the group was twofold:
(a) to provide a means for social interaction with peers and (b) to
provide a way to deal with aging issues such as retirement. To the
surprise of the staff, the hottest topic at the first session was the subject
of death. Specifically, participants were interested in reporting if they
had experienced the death of someone close to them. Staff suggested
that for the second meeting each person bring in pictures of deceased
family members, share the pictures with the group, and talk about
these family members. This second meeting was very well-received.
Even people with more severe disabilities and some who frequently
were hesitant to participate in groups became involved. The group
continued to meet for its original purpose. Participants did not obsess
or dwell on the subject of death. It was the perception of staff that
bereaved individuals had determined who else had similar experiences
and tended to connect with these individuals for peer support.

92. *Look for opportunities where the bereaved person can
help others* **(Instruct/Teach/Model; Support from Others).** After
the person has gone through the initial stages of grief, it may boost the

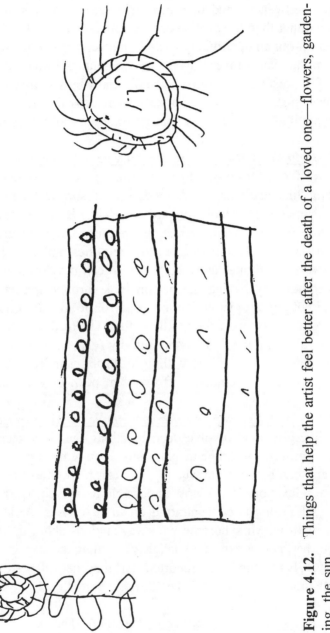

Figure 4.12. Things that help the artist feel better after the death of a loved one—flowers, gardening, the sun.

person's self-esteem and help him or her focus on his or her own abilities rather than losses if he or she can help others. The individual might seek out an opportunity to do volunteer work. For example, he or she might visit, deliver flowers, or hand out cold water at a nursing home. The person could help others informally by assisting a coworker with learning a task, assisting a staff member with a special project, or completing a task at home that he or she usually does not do.

93. *Help the person choose and engage in a new leisure activity* **(Support from Others).** After the initial pain and commotion surrounding the death have subsided, the person will benefit from having something to look forward to. Help identify a new leisure activity to try. Therapeutic recreation therapists and occupational therapists have lists of numerous leisure activities and may have pictures of these activities as well. You also can develop a package of such activities by having the person look through magazines with you and cutting out pictures. Ask the person to identify one or more activities that look as if they will be fun. Try to establish a regular schedule for the person to try this activity (e.g., once a week). Identify someone who would be willing to do the activity with the person (e.g., a family member, staff member, peer, or volunteer).

94. *Help the person learn some simple yoga exercises* **(Physical).** Exercises that involve deep breathing, gentle stretching, and repetitive movement can be taught easily, require no expensive equipment, and can be done anywhere. They can help relieve tension and promote relaxation. It is almost impossible to actively worry or hold tension while one is concentrating on the exercises. A 44-year-old woman with Down syndrome who was anxious about the declining health of her mother expressed delight at learning the exercises. "These are easy. This is fun." She reported that they helped her during the difficult time as her mother's health deteriorated.

95. *Promote physical activity* **(Physical).** The person will feel better physically and emotionally if he or she engages in physical activity on a regular basis. Determine what physical activity would

be appealing to the person—walking, jogging, using a treadmill or exercise bike, aerobic dance, swimming, etc. The person will be much more likely to engage in the activity and continue to do it if you participate with him or her or find someone else who will do so on a regular basis. Your local Special Olympics office can provide you with information about Special Olympics activities and may be able to recommend other groups that promote and provide opportunities for physical activities.

96. *Help identify people who will communicate regularly with the bereaved individual by sending greeting cards, sending pictures, and possibly making a couple of telephone calls per year* **(Support from Others).** Consider contacting or helping the bereaved person contact extended family members, current or former neighbors and family friends, favorite staff members, or former staff members. Alert them that a greeting card, letter, picture, or phone call would help the bereaved person feel less lonely. This may be particularly valuable if the deceased had communicated regularly with the bereaved individual in these ways and thus the bereaved person is likely to sorely miss this type of interaction.

97. *Help the person plant and maintain a butterfly garden* **(Nature/Outdoors; Physical).** There is a variety of flowers and shrubs that are likely to attract butterflies. Consult gardening books or staff at a local greenhouse to identify these plants and to determine which are likely to grow well in your area. Some to consider include: verbena, lantana, bee balm, black-eyed susan, butterfly bush, butterfly milkweed, coneflower, garden phlox, heliotrope, lavender, pincushion flower, showy stonecrop, and sweet william. Help plant a butterfly garden in remembrance of the person who died. Some people have found comfort in this activity because of the spirit-like nature of butterflies and the symbolism associated with the "death" of the caterpillar and its "rebirth" as a butterfly. If a garden plot is not feasible, nature and educational stores and catalogs often carry butterfly kits, which contain caterpillars and the equipment necessary to promote their change into butterflies.

98. *Spend time in a park-like setting* (**Nature/Outdoors; Physical**). Walking in a soothing, natural setting can help an individual who is grieving. The activity of walking uses the large muscles in the arms and legs; this is excellent exercise and helps release tension that someone may be holding in the body. The rhythm of walking can release the mind to drift and access memories or emotions of which the person may not be aware. Walking in a setting that is soothing, particularly in a woods or park-like area, can help someone get in touch with the natural flow of life, growth, death and rejuvenation. When the person visits this place repeatedly, he or she can see the changes in the environment from season to season. The individual can see the fresh green of new growth in the spring that gives hope after a long period of winter. He or she can feel the changes in the air, the texture of the ground beneath, or the fullness or absence of bird and animal activity surrounding him or her. You can point out that even on the bleakest wintry day, a bird sings and the warmth of the sun can provide comfort.

99. *Help the person assume a previous role or task of the deceased person* (**Instruct/Teach/Model; Physical; Ritual/Tradition**). Talk with the bereaved person and identify the tasks or roles that the deceased had performed (e.g., taking out the trash, sending greeting cards to family members at birthdays and holidays, making the coffee in the morning, and so forth). The bereaved person may want to choose one or more of these tasks to do. This is both practical (someone may have to do these tasks) as well as therapeutic (it may feel very good for the bereaved person to do something that always had been done by the deceased person).

100. *Plant a memory garden or grow specific plants in pots that have special meaning* (**Nature/Outdoors; Physical; Ritual/Tradition**). This can be done in several ways. Someone might grow plants that were favorites of the deceased individual. Or the person might grow plants with symbolic names or legends, such as forget-me-nots, bleeding hearts, or rosemary, which is known as the herb of remembrance. Others could be identified through garden stores or catalogs.

101. *Help the person sew a quilt in memory of the deceased person* (**Creative Arts; Ritual/Tradition**). The design and colors could be influenced by preferences of the deceased (e.g., What were the deceased's favorite colors? What design would the person have liked?). Perhaps the bereaved person would like to include the name and favorite sayings of the deceased in the design. Identify what parts of the quilt the bereaved person could make. Enlist the help of other people who might enjoy supporting the bereaved individual by working on this project with him or her.

102. *Encourage and help the person utilize a calendar as a way to look forward to upcoming events* (**Instruct/Teach/Model; Support from Others**). The person will need to grieve but also to begin to look forward to the future. One way to help with this is to use a calendar to mark upcoming events that will be positive for the bereaved person. If there is a month in which special events are missing, help him or her schedule some (e.g., to invite friends over for a dessert that the bereaved has made or chosen from a bakery, or to invite someone over to watch an athletic event on television and serve special snacks and beverages).

103. *Provide death education* (**Instruct/Teach/Model**). The death of someone close is likely to trigger thoughts of one's own eventual death. If the bereaved person is someone who has been sheltered from this topic, he or she may benefit from education or training on this topic. Some agencies that serve adults or children with developmental disabilities may have training programs for this purpose. Other resources for how to go about providing this education could be gleaned from personnel at hospice agencies, from teachers or social workers who provide death education for students, from children's books explaining death, and from chapter 5 of this book, "Professional Assistance."

104. *Help the person locate musical organizations in which he or she could participate* (**Music**). As the bereaved person starts moving on with life, it will be important to identify social activities in

which he or she can participate. If musically inclined, the person might enjoy participating in a musical organization such as a church choir or Very Special Arts choir.

105. *Visit a nature store with the bereaved person* (**Nature/ Outdoors; Ritual/Tradition**). There are many examples of loss and renewal in nature: the change of seasons, planting, harvesting, the life cycle of different creatures in the animal kingdom. You may want to purchase items together that seem to have special meaning for the person with mental retardation. Purchases to consider include books, seeds, calendars, posters, stuffed animals, or puppets (e.g., there are some that demonstrate a change from one form to another —a caterpillar that unzips, turns inside out, and becomes a butterfly, and a tadpole that turns into a frog).

106. *Help the person make a decorative wreath using silk replicas of the deceased person's favorite flowers* (**Creative Arts**). Possible tasks involved in this project include deciding on what colors and season to focus (e.g., flowers from the favorite season of the person who died might be chosen), visiting a craft store to pick out the flowers, planning the design, putting the wreath together, and deciding where to hang the wreath. When completed, the bereaved will have something tangible and pretty to remind him or her of the loved one.

107. *Use a candle ritual to help explain the concept of "letting go and moving on with life"* (**Ritual/Tradition**). See Jewett (1982, pp. 17-18) for the original description of this ritual.

In sum, the helper uses candles to represent love as love and loss are demonstrated. The helper might say something such as, "When you were born, you had the gift to give love and to get love. This gift is like a light; it makes you feel warm and happy." The helper then will light a candle representing the bereaved person. Then other candles are lit for other people in the family (e.g., the mother, father, and siblings), and one is lit for the deceased. The helper can say a few words about each member of the family such as, "Your mother and father knew you first; they loved you very much." Then the helper can mention the circumstances of the death. The candle representing the deceased can be moved across the room or extinguished, depending on the religious beliefs of the bereaved. The helper can talk about how life has changed for the bereaved since the death. He or she can talk about the possibility of new people coming into the life of the bereaved person—a new friend, a new staff person, a relative who is becoming more involved. The helper can light additional candles for the other people in the bereaved person's life. The helper also can demonstrate that the first candle is still burning. He or she can say something such as, "The important thing for you to remember is that the light of love you feel for your dad [name the deceased person] will not go out. Loving is not like soup that you dish up until it is all gone. You can love as many people as you get close to. But no one will make you blow out any of your candles." The person can be helped to understand that he or she will still have a candle lit "in his [or her] heart" for the deceased.

Symbolic rituals such as this one can be very powerful. Take care to allow plenty of time in conducting it and to end it very carefully. Explain to the bereaved that of course the candles are not really people but that they help us think about people. It is now time to put out the candles, but that does not mean that he or she will stop loving the deceased when the candle is extinguished. The helper also can mention that, instead of using a candle, the bereaved can remember the person who died with his or her mind and heart. Ask the bereaved person if he or she is ready for the candles to be blown out and whether that is to be done by you or by the bereaved person. Do this procedure with each candle that was lit. Flashlights could be used if safety issues or building regulations do not allow the use of candles.

108. _Be alert for different helping techniques or design others based on your knowledge of the bereaved person_ (**All Categories**). Please remember that the ideas that have been described here are

just the tip of the iceberg. They are ideas that the authors have used or heard about, or that the authors expect to be helpful to others. You are encouraged to dialogue with professionals and families who have coped with the loss of a loved one and to use your own creativity and knowledge of the bereaved person to locate or develop other ideas to help the person as he or she grieves.

PROFESSIONAL ASSISTANCE

WARNING SIGNS TO DETERMINE
WHEN TO SEEK HELP

Rando (1993) provided a detailed description of warning signs and complicating factors in grieving. The following are some signs that will help you determine if professional help should be sought.

Experiencing Multiple Losses

Two situations can lead to multiple losses: when more than one person dies or when there is more than one type of loss. In the first situation, multiple deaths of friends, housemates, or relatives can tax someone's ability to cope (see Figure 5.1). In the second situation, significant life changes following a death may create additional losses for the bereaved person (e.g., a change in residence, community, finances, and people available to provide support). Both situations may result in grief overload. In grief overload, a person may begin to shut down and become incapacitated in one or more significant areas of life.

Figure 5.1. The artist is overwhelmed by multiple deaths. The losses (Mom, Dad, Ann) "fill up" the box.

Idealizing the Deceased

To fully grieve the loss of a loved one, people need to remember and talk about both the positive and the negative aspects of the deceased person's personality and habits. If the bereaved continually only dwells on the positive aspects, it may be an indication that he or she is "stuck" in the grieving process.

Continuing to Inappropriately Act Out Grief over Time

Some people do not know how to express their emotions appropriately regarding a death. Instead, the sorrow, anger, and upset that they feel comes out in inappropriate or harmful ways. A grief counselor, particularly someone adept at using art, music, or alternative ways to express feelings, can help affirm, express, and change how these feelings are expressed.

Using Alcohol and/or Other Drugs to Cope

The use of alcohol or other drugs is often an attempt to get relief from the strong emotions of grief. Prolonged use only delays the healing process, however, and may result in another difficulty—addiction.

Talking about Suicide

Talk about suicide always should be given serious attention and assessment by a competent professional. It is not unusual for those who are grieving to express the desire to be reunited with the deceased or to express the desire to be dead also because they feel overwhelmed by everything with which they must cope. This is different from the actual intention to kill oneself. This distinction needs to be made by someone trained to do so.

Developing Physical Symptoms of the Person Who Was Ill and Died

Physical symptoms should be treated seriously, and the possibility of an actual illness should be ruled out by a physician. If physical symptoms identical to those of the person who died persist without medical evidence, this may be an indicator of complicated grieving and, if so, professional intervention is warranted.

Experiencing Sleep Deprivation

Sleep disturbances are a normal part of grieving. When someone is unable to sleep for prolonged periods of time, however, he or she may become sleep deprived. Sleep deprivation affects the person's health, further complicates the person's life, and should be remedied. Often drugs are prescribed for a *short time* to help the grieving person resume more normal sleep patterns and get some rest.

Having a Problematic Relationship with the Deceased in the Past

One might assume that a person would not be deeply upset if he or she did not have a good relationship with the deceased; however, just the reverse can be true. Worden (1982) stated, "The most frequent type of relationship that hinders people from adequately grieving is the highly ambivalent one." The bereaved individual may feel a lot of anger or guilt in this circumstance. If this appears to be the case, the person is likely to benefit from professional assistance.

Experiencing a Death Loss that Was Sudden and Unexpected or Associated with Stigma

The need for professional assistance may be increased if the death was a traumatic one or if it is viewed by some as having a stigma attached (e.g., an accident, suicide, homicide, or death resulting from AIDS).

INDICATIONS THAT PROFESSIONAL ASSISTANCE IS NEEDED

To determine if you need to seek professional help for someone who is grieving consider the following:

- the length of time the person has been grieving,
- the intensity of the grief reactions, and
- any warning signs that indicate potential difficulties.

If these seem longer and stronger than what you would expect, consider consulting with a professional. If you have any doubt at all, it may be a good idea to contact a qualified professional for an assessment. Early intervention can make a significant difference in the grief response of people mourning a death loss and can help them better handle other losses that they may encounter in their lives.

WHERE TO GO FOR PROFESSIONAL ASSISTANCE

A number of organizations provide grief counseling or can refer you to qualified bereavement counselors. Some are listed here. Counselors and therapists have a wide variety of credentials (e.g., bereavement counselor, pastoral counselor, social worker, psychologist) and may work in a variety of settings (e.g., a hospice, hospital, church, clinic, mental health center, or private practice). It is a good idea to inquire about the background of a counselor or therapist to be certain that the person has had *training and experience in the area of grief.* It is also important to determine if the counselor or therapist is someone with whom the bereaved individual can enjoy trust and feel comfortable.

A good resource for locating such help in your community is a self-help group that deals with death loss. Members usually know of local counselors and therapists with good reputations in the grief field. Three of these support groups are listed below. Typically, your local hospice organization will know if there are additional resources.

National Organizations

The National Hospice Organization (NHO)
1901 North Moore Street
Suite 901
Arlington, VA 22209

phone: (800) 658-8898 to obtain a local hospice number
phone: (703) 243-5900 general office number
e-mail: drsnho@cais.com
web site: www.nho.org

This national organization can give you the name and number of the hospice in your area that can be contacted for help. Hospice staff work with people who have terminal illnesses and their families. Some also have community outreach programs to assist others who may be grieving a death loss. Hospice agencies across the country vary greatly in size and available services. If a hospice is unable to provide you with help itself because of its size or mission, it still may be an excellent resource for referral to counselors, therapists, and other groups in your community.

Association for Death Education and Counseling (ADEC)
638 Prospect Avenue
Hartford, CT 06105-4250

phone: (860) 586-7503
FAX: (860) 586-7550
e-mail: info@adec.org
web site: www.adec.org

ADEC promotes education about death loss, grief, and grief counseling nationwide. The organization provides a certification program for Grief Counselors and Death Educators, and maintains a registry of those who have maintained their certification. There are about 500 persons certified nationwide. ADEC provides free referrals to someone in your community.

National Association for Music Therapy (NAMT)
8455 Colesville Road, Suite 1000
Silver Spring, MD 20910

phone: (301) 589-3300
FAX: (301) 589-5175
e-mail: info@namt.com
web site: www.namt.com\namt\

NAMT supports the therapeutic use of music in hospital, rehabilitation, educational, and community settings. There are over 5,000 music therapists employed throughout the U.S. NAMT regulates the clinical practice of music therapy to insure that services provided to persons with disabilities are the highest quality possible. NAMT will do a search by zip code and can provide you with names of music therapists in your geographical area. They first will ask you to identify the reason for your inquiry. Explain to them that you are looking for a music therapist who can work with an adult with mental retardation who is grieving.

American Art Therapy Association, Inc. (AATA)
1202 Allanson Road
Mundelein, IL 60060

phone: (847) 949-6064
FAX: (847) 566-4580
e-mail: estygariii@aol.com
web site: www.arttherapy.org

AATA is an organization of professionals dedicated to the belief that the creative process involved in the making of art is healing and life enhancing. Its mission is to serve its members and the general public by providing standards of professional competence, and developing and promoting knowledge in, and of, the field of art therapy. Members of AATA have master's degrees and are registered. There are chapter offices in most states. If you are looking for an art therapist, you can call the outpatient mental health center or the psychiatry department of your local clinic or hospital for names of art therapists in your area. You also can call the national office of AATA; they will give you the number of the chapter in your state.

National Support Groups

The Compassionate Friends - National Office
P.O. Box 3696
Oak Brook, IL 60522-3696

phone: (630) 990-0010
FAX: (630) 990-0246
e-mail: TCF_National@prodigy.com
web site: www.jjt.com\~tcf_national

Compassionate Friends is a support organization for people who are dealing with the death of a child of any age. They can provide the number of your local chapter, if one exists in your area, and may be able to refer you to a qualified professional.

Survivors of Suicide - National Office (SOS)
Suicide Prevention Center, Inc.
184 Salem Avenue
Dayton, Ohio 45406

phone: (937) 297-4777
FAX: (937) 298-4310
e-mail: none
web site: none

SOS is a nationwide support group for people surviving the trauma of a suicide. This group also can refer you to a local chapter, which would be likely to know qualified professionals in your area.

American Association of Retired Persons (AARP)
Widowed Persons Service
601 E Street, N.W.
Washington, D.C. 20049

phone: (202) 434-2260
FAX: (202) 434-6474
e-mail: aarp.org
web site: www.aarp.org

Widowed Persons Service is a nationwide support group for widows and widowers. They can provide written materials and re-ferrals to local chapters.

REFERENCES

Boulden, J., & Boulden, J. (1992). *Saying goodbye.* Weaverville, CA: Boulden Publishing.

Bowlby, J. (1980). *Attachment and loss: Loss, sadness and depression* (volume III). New York: BasicBooks.

Braza, K. (1992). *Memory book for bereaved children.* Salt Lake City, UT: Healing Resources.

Buscaglia, L. (1982). *The fall of Freddie the leaf.* New York: Henry Holt & Co.

Cook, A. S., & Dworkin, D. S. (1992). *Helping the bereaved: Therapeutic interventions for children, adolescents, and adults.* New York: BasicBooks.

Deits, B. (1988). *Life after loss: A personal guide dealing with death, divorce, job change and relocation.* Tucson, AZ: Fisher Books.

Deutsch, H. (1985). Grief counseling with the mentally retarded clients. *Psychiatric Aspects of Mental Retardation Reviews, 4*(5), 17-20.

Dougy Center (The). (1990). *Waving good-bye: An activities manual for children in grief.* Portland, OR: Author.

Emberley, E. (1977). *Ed Emberley's great thumbprint drawing book.* Boston: Little, Brown and Company.

Emerson, P. (1977). Covert grief reaction in mentally retarded clients. *Mental Retardation, 15*(6), 46-47.

Feil, N. (1993). *The validation breakthrough: Simple techniques for communicating with people with "Alzheimer's -type dementia."* Baltimore, MD: Health Professions Press.

Grollman, E. A. (1996). Spiritual support after sudden loss. In K. J. Doka (Ed.), *Living with grief after sudden loss* (pp. 185-188). Washington, DC: Hospice Foundation of America.

Harper, D. C., & Wadsworth, J. S. (1993). Grief in adults with mental retardation: Preliminary findings. *Research in Developmental Disabilities, 14,* 313-330.

Hedger, C. J., & Dyer Smith, M. J. (1993). Death education for older adults with developmental disabilities: A life cycle therapeutic recreation approach. *Activities, Adaptation & Aging 18*(1), 29-36.

Heegaard, M. (1988). *When someone very special dies: Children can learn to cope with grief.* Minneapolis, MN: Woodland Press.

Howell, M. C. (Ed.). (1989). *Serving the underserved: Caring for people who are both old and mentally retarded.* Boston: Exceptional Parent Press.

Irish, D. P., Lundquist, K. F., & Jenkins Nelsen, V. (1993). *Ethnic variations in dying, death, and grief: Diversity in universality.* Washington, DC: Taylor & Francis.

Jewett, C. (1982). *Helping children cope with separation and loss.* Harvard, MA: The Harvard Common Press.

Kauffman, J. (1994). Mourning and mental retardation. *Death Studies, 18,* 257-271.

Kloeppel, D. A., & Hollins, S. (1989). Double handicap: Mental retardation and death in the family. *Death Studies, 13,* 31-38.

Lindemann, E. (1944). Symptomatology and management of acute grief. *American Journal of Psychiatry, 101,* 141-148.

McDaniel, B. A. (1989). A group work experience with mentally retarded adults on the issues of death and dying. *Journal of Gerontological Social Work, 13*(3/4), 187-191.

Marquardt, H. A. (1989). Funeral and memorial services. In M. C. Howell (Ed.), *Serving the underserved: Caring for people who are both old and mentally retarded* (pp. 346-348). Boston: Exceptional Parent Press.

Moise, L. E. (1978). In sickness and in death. *Mental Retardation, 16*(6), 397-398.

Pima Council on Developmental Disabilities. (1994). *More years, more tears: How grief and loss experiences affect adults with mental retardation* [videotape—length 39:32]. Tucson, AZ: Author.

Rando, T. A. (1993). *Treatment of complicated mourning.* Champaign, IL: Research Press.

Rosenblatt, P. C. (1988). Grief: The social context of private feelings. *Journal of Social Issues, 44*(3), 67-78.

Rosenblatt, P. C. (1993). Cross-cultural variation in the experience, expression, and understanding of grief. In D. P. Irish, K. F. Lundquist,

& V. Jenkins Nelsen (Eds.), *Ethnic variations in dying, death, and grief: Diversity in universality* (pp. 13-19). Washington, DC: Taylor & Francis.

Rosenblatt, P., & Elde, C. (1990). Shared reminiscence about a deceased parent: Implications for grief education and grief counseling. *Family Relations, 39,* 206-210.

Rothenberg, E. D. (1994). Bereavement intervention with vulnerable populations: A case report on group work with the developmentally disabled. *Social Work with Groups, 17*(3), 61-75.

Sigelman, C. K., Budd, E. C., Winder, J. L., Schoenrock, C. J., & Martin, P. W. (1982). Evaluating alternative techniques of questioning mentally retarded persons. *American Journal of Mental Deficiency, 86,* 511-518.

Simos, B. G. (1979). *A time to grieve: Loss as a universal human experience.* New York: Family Service Association of America.

Staudacher, C. (1991). *Men & grief: A guide for men surviving the death of a loved one—A resource for caregivers and mental health professionals.* Oakland, CA: New Harbinger Publications.

Tatelbaum, J. (1980). *The courage to grieve.* New York: Harper & Row.

Tatelbaum, J. (1989). *You don't have to suffer: A handbook for moving beyond life's crises.* New York: Harper & Row.

Weizman, S. G., & Kamm, P. (1985). *About mourning: Support and guidance for the bereaved.* New York: Human Sciences Press.

Worden, J. W. (1982). *Grief counseling and grief therapy: A handbook for the mental health practitioner.* New York: Springer Publishing Co.

INDEX

alcohol, coping and use of,
    101
anger, 7
    death and expression of, 57

behavior, grieving and change
    in, 18, 21, 31

candle ritual, 78, 96–97
caregivers
    comforting of mentally-
        retarded grieving adult,
        33–34
    death announcement to
        mentally-retarded adult,
        28–31
    focus on mentally-retarded
        adult's abilities, 89, 90,
        92
    help with mentally-retarded

adult's coping, 35–36,
    44, 49, 57–59, 72, 88–
    89
    own grieving and support to
        mentally-disabled adult,
        52–53
    support through presence,
        50, 52
    support to bereaved person,
        1, 4
    support to mentally-retarded
        grieving adult, 17, 22–
        23, 28
cemetery, visits to, 77–78
children, death and, 16
cognitive difficulties, 16–17
contribution, tribute to the
    deceased through material,
    71–72
creative arts
    acceptance of loss through,
        45–46, 82, 84

creative arts (*Cont.*)
  expression of feeling
    through, 57, 59–60, 66,
    71

dance, expression of feeling
    through, 73
death
  announcement to mentally-
    retarded adult, 29–30
  children and, 16
  discussion of feelings about,
    72–73
  education, 95
  idealization of the deceased,
    101
  openness about, 28–31, 44
  sudden/stigma associated,
    102
  teaching severely disabled
    adult about, 49–50
  understanding and feeling of
    loss, 16–17, 31–33
  use of books to explain, 53–
    54
drugs, coping and use of, 101

emotional energy
  reinvestment of, 5
  strategies for reinvestment
    of, 90–98
emotions. *See also* feeling
  expression of, 17
environment
  grieving and adjustment to, 5

strategies to help adjustment
  to, 73–89
ethnic background, expression
  of grief and, 4

family member, mentally-
  retarded adult's grief and,
  22–23, 75
feeling. *See also* emotions
  death and mentally-retarded
    adult's expression of,
    31–33, 54–58
feeling different, 10–11
funeral/memorial service
  acceptance of loss by
    attendance to, 46–48
  mentally-retarded adult's
    involvement with
    arrangements of, 44–47
future, mentally-retarded
  grieving adult's, 95

gender, grieving emotions and,
  4
grief
  duration, 13–14
  pain experience, 2–4, 39–40
  professional help and, 103
  reactions to, 8–9
  triggers, 14
guilt, 7, 10
  problematic relationship
    with the deceased and,
    102

healing, survivor's, 5–6

image of the diseased, experi-
    ence with, 11–12

journal, adjustment to loss by
    keeping a, 80

leisure activity, adjustment to
    loss through new, 92
loss(es)
    acceptance of reality of, 2
    multiple, 24–25, 99–100
    strategies to help acceptance
        of, 43–50
    understanding death and
        feeling of, 16–17

memories
    adjustment to loss through
        sharing of, 86
    creation of object as keeper
        of, 79–82
    rocks/shells/collection as
        symbolic, 81–82
    selection of one of the
        deceased's belonging
        as, 76
metaphors, grief and use of, 3
mourning
    feeling a year after the
        death, 89
    tasks, 2, 27

music
    adjustment to loss through,
        80, 83–84, 95–96
    expression of feeling
        through, 71–72

nature. *See also* water
    adjustment to loss through
        communing with, 93,
        94
    as a source of comfort, 70
    tree/garden planting as
        memorial, 90, 93–94

pain. *See also* somatic distress
    physical grief, 3, 8, 13, 102
    strategies to help relief of
        grief, 50–73
perseveration, retelling grief
    symptom *vs.*, 34
photographs, adjustment to
    loss and use of, 75, 77
physical activity, adjustment to
    loss through, 92
prayer, grieving and, 60–66
professional assistance
    criteria for seeking, 103
    sources of, 104–107

regression, 11
resources, mentally-retarded
    adult's lack of, 25
restlessness, 10

ritual. *See also* candle ritual;
prayer
anniversary, 87–88
dinners, 78
expression of feeling
through, 70
grieving and, 68–69
support from, 12
routine, loss of daily, 11

sadness, 7
positive response to, 18
sleep deprivation, 102
social support, mentally-
retarded adult's grief and,
23–24
somatic distress, 10
spiritual quest, 12
adjustment to loss through,
92
story-telling, adjustment to loss
through, 86

strategies, knowledge of
grieving person and
caregiver's, 39, 43
suicide, grief and, 101
support
mentally-retarded adult's
grief process and, 28,
44, 75–76
mentally-retarded adult's
loss of lifelong, 25–26
mentally-retarded grieving
adult and buddies,' 77
support group, 75–76, 90

video/movie watching, adjustment to loss through, 85

water, as a source of comfort,
67–68
written words, comfort
through, 58

ABOUT THE AUTHORS

Charlene Luchterhand, M.S.S.W., CICSW, is a certified independent clinical social worker. She has a B.A. in social work and sociology and a M.S.S.W., all from the University of Wisconsin-Madison. Ms. Luchterhand's career includes experience in aging, developmental disabilities, health care, higher education, and mental health.

Ms. Luchterhand was the Coordinator of the Program on Aging & Developmental Disabilities, Waisman Center University Affiliated Program, at the University of Wisconsin-Madison for eight years. She managed an Aging & Developmental Disabilities Clinic and provided outreach education for a variety of national, state, and local audiences. She was a member of the Management Team for the Wisconsin Life-Long Planning Initiative for Older Adults with Developmental Disabilities and a member of the International Work Group on Alzheimer's Disease and Mental Retardation.

Ms. Luchterhand is currently with the Dean Foundation for Health, Research, and Education in Middleton, Wisconsin. She serves on the Board of Directors of R.F.D.F, a non-profit agency providing residential services to aging adults and those with disabilities, and she is a member of the Wisconsin Coalition on Mental Health, Substance Abuse, and Aging. She continues to work on behalf of adults with mental retardation who are grieving. She resides with her husband, Randall, and several companion animals in rural Dane County, Wisconsin.

Nancy E. Murphy, M.Ed., LPC, is a psychotherapist in private practice with Psychology Associates in Madison, Wisconsin. She has a B.A. from Indiana University in Bloomington and a M.Ed. in Counseling from the University of Missouri-St. Louis. She is a Licensed Professional Counselor specializing in therapy with children, adolescents, and people with disabilities. Her career includes experience in mental health, rehabilitation, hospice, grief and bereavement, expressive therapies, and brain injury. She has provided expertise on grief and grieving for national and state conferences, medical facilities, schools, and businesses.

Membership and roles in various organizations have included: Consultant at the Waisman Center, University Affiliated Program, University of Wisconsin-Madison; Field Supervisor at the University of Wisconsin-Madison School of Social Work; Member of the Dane County Grief Resource Group; President of the St. Louis Chapter, National Rehabilitation Association; Board Member of the Missouri Association of Rehabilitation Facilities; Board Member of the Vocational Transition Council of St. Louis; Advisory Council Member of the Malcolm Bliss State Hospital, St. Louis.

Ms. Murphy resides in Madison, Wisconsin, with her husband, Bob, and her stepdaughter, Shanti.